"Scott Kelby nails the joys and f[...]
in a PC world (though Scott's writi[...]
you'll cry, you'll shout, 'Amen.' Bu. , ...
—*and know you're in the company of a kindred spirit."*
DENNIS SELLERS
MacCentral.com

"My three favorite writers about the Macintosh experience are
Guy Kawasaki, Andy Ihnatko, and Scott Kelby. Scott has the unusual
ability to channel his excitement and frustration into humor and
clarity that makes me laugh while he makes me think."
JAY NELSON
Editor & Publisher, *Design Tools Monthly*

"Filled with insightful wit and outrageous comedy, Macintosh...The Naked Truth
will have you in stitches. A must-read for any Macintosh enthusiast."
STAN FLACK
President/Publisher, MacMinute.com

"This is a book all Mac users should read! Scott speaks up for the average
Mac user and says publicly what we've all said privately. It's a great read!"
SHAWN KING
The Mac Show Live

"A fun read I'm sure all Mac users can relate to. I laughed out loud thinking
'yeah, that happened to me too.' If you own a Mac, you should read this book."
KURT CHRISTENSEN
VersionTracker

"Kelby is one sick puppy. I loved it! If you're a Mac fan, put
Macintosh...The Naked Truth *on your 'must-read' list."*
BOB "DR. MAC" LEVITUS
Best-selling author of *Dr. Mac: The OS X Files* and
Mac OS X For Dummies (and a rabid Mac fan for more than 15 years).

"...had me laughing out loud and crying real tears. This is a
must-have book for any Mac veteran and is not for the faint of heart."
TERRY WHITE
President & Founder MacGroup–Detroit

Macintosh...
The Naked Truth

Scott Kelby

Macintosh... The naked truth

The "Naked Truth" Team:

EDITOR
Richard Theriault

PRODUCTION EDITOR
Chris Main

COPY EDITOR
Barbara Thompson

TYPE TWEAKING
Dave Damstra

COVER DESIGN
Felix Nelson

SITE DESIGN
Stacy Behan

The New Riders Team:

PUBLISHER
David Dwyer

ASSOCIATE PUBLISHER
Stephanie Wall

EXECUTIVE EDITOR
Steve Weiss

MANAGING EDITOR
Sarah Kearns

PRODUCTION
Jeff Bredensteiner

PROOFREADER
Lisa Stumpf

PUBLISHED BY
New Riders Publishing

Copyright © 2002 by New Riders Publishing

FIRST EDITION: March 2002

International Standard Book Number: 0-7357-1284-0

Library of Congress Catalog Card Number: 2002100322

06 05 04 03 02   7 6 5 4 3 2

Interpretation of the printing code: The rightmost double-digit number is the year of the book's printing; the rightmost single-digit number is the number of the book's printing. For example, the printing code 02-1 shows that the first printing of the book occurred in 2002.

Composed in Helvetica Black and Minion by KW Media Group

Printed in the United States of America

Trademarks
All terms mentioned in this book that are known to be trademarks or service marks have been appropriately capitalized. New Riders Publishing cannot attest to the accuracy of this information. Use of a term in the book should not be regarded as affecting the validity of any trademark or service mark.

Macintosh, iBook, iMovie, iPod, iPhoto, PowerBook, PowerMac, Studio Display, and QuickTime are all registered trademarks of Apple Computer, Inc.

Windows is a registered trademark of Microsoft Corporation.

All brand names and product names used in this book are tradenames, service marks, trademarks, or registered trademarks of their respective owners.

Warning and Disclaimer
This book is designed to provide information for Apple Macintosh users. Every effort has been made to make this book as complete and as accurate as possible, but no warranty of fitness is implied.

For Kalebra.
I just can't imagine
loving anyone but her.

Table of **contents**

About the author

Scott Kelby

Scott is Editor-in-Chief of *Mac Design Magazine,* the graphics magazine for Macintosh users, and *Photoshop User* magazine, the Adobe® Photoshop® "How-to" magazine. Scott is co-founder of *Mac Today* magazine, and has been a contributing editor and columnist to several Mac Web sites, including MacCentral.com.

He is president of the National Association of Photoshop Professionals (NAPP), the worldwide trade association for Adobe Photoshop users, and is President of KW Media Group, Inc., a Florida-based software education and publishing firm.

Author of the best-selling books *Photoshop 6 Down & Dirty Tricks* and *Photoshop 6 Photo-Retouching Secrets,* Scott is also co-author of *Photoshop 6 Killer Tips,* all from New Riders Publishing.

He's a contributing author to the books *Maclopedia, the Ultimate Reference on Everything Macintosh* from Hayden Books; *Photoshop 6 Effects Magic* from New Riders; and *Adobe Web Design and Publishing Unleashed* from Sams.net Publishing.

Scott is training Director for the Adobe Photoshop Seminar Tour, Technical Chair for PhotoshopWorld, and is a speaker at graphics trade shows and events around the world, including Macworld Expo. He is also featured in a series of Photoshop, Illustrator, and Web design video training tapes and has been training Macintosh graphics professionals around the world since 1993.

Scott lives in the Tampa Bay area of Florida with his wife Kalebra and his 5-year-old son Jordan. For more background info on him, visit www.scottkelby.com.

Acknowledgments

Perhaps the greatest gift I've been blessed with is to be surrounded by such talented, amazing, and absolutely wonderful people, without whom this book would not have been possible.

First, I'd like to thank my amazing wife Kalebra. Her limitless energy is only matched by her beauty; her genuine enthusiasm for life is only matched by her heart. She always knows just what to say, and just when to say it, and her wit and marvelous sense of humor have made these past 14 years an absolute pleasure. To me, she is proof without a doubt that fairy tales do come true.

I'm particularly delighted to acknowledge the book's editor (and my good friend of many years) Richard Theriault. Dick was my first full-time editor at *Mac Today* magazine, and anything that was good in it, he had a hand in. Dick retired a few years back to play with his grandchildren, so it took a bit of coaxing (and lightly veiled threats of physical violence) to get him to take this project on, but I wasn't going to have it any other way. Dick is a first-class wordsmith, a true gentleman, and a Macintosh fanatic to the core. It's an honor and privilege to have him edit this book.

I want to thank my creative team who worked at a "ludicrous speed," including my creative director Felix Nelson, for pulling yet another rabbit out of his hat. To my Production Editor Chris Main, for doing all the thankless work and for his excellent suggestions along the way. To Barbara Thompson for putting a magnifying glass on the text, and to Dave Damstra, for once again "Damstracizing" the pages into a very "cleanly" state. To my assistant Gina "Yo Gina" Profitt, for keeping a lot of plates in the air while I was writing this book. To Stacy Behan, who doesn't know it yet, but will be doing a wonderful job on the book's Web site, and to everyone at KW Media Group for defining what teamwork is all about.

Thanks to my business partner and friend Jim Workman, who encouraged me to write this book, and whose uncanny memory helped with some of the research. Also thanks to Dave Gales, who helped come up with the name for the book and broke a writer's logjam that got the project off the ground. Also, thanks to Dave Moser for all his help, guidance, and enthusiasm for the project.

I want to thank all my Mac friends, whose ideas, rantings, jokes, and joys had a very profound effect on this book, including Rod "Mac Daddy" Harlan, Bill Carroll, Don Wiggins, Jim Patterson, Jim Goodman, Jeff Hemmel, Dianne Coman, Terry "T-bone" White, Don Crabb, Geoff Harriman, Rye Livingston, Bill Lindsay, John Graden, Mike O'Berry, John Couch, Larry Becker, Ed Pace, and thanks to Guy Kawasaki for bringing out the Mac evangelist in all of us.

The wonderful publishing team at New Riders deserves special credit, and in particular Steve Weiss. He had to pitch this Mac book to a boardroom of PC-using editors. Although he never let on, I'm sure they weren't like "Great! A book that makes fun of us!" yet he was able to overcome all of that and convince them to take a leap of faith and publish a computer book that isn't about how to use a computer. It takes a special company to do that, and I'm indebted to both Steve and David Dwyer for having the courage and vision to take a chance on a book "for the rest of us."

A special thanks goes to my son Jordan (my little buddy) who would see me writing and always ask "Can I work with you, Daddy?" His version of work is my stopping writing, launching Photoshop, and drawing the Iron Giant robot for him—but I wouldn't have it any other way.

I want to thank my father for teaching me the value of honesty, for teaching me how to say "I'm sorry," for always showing his love and affection for me, and for always letting me know how proud he is of my accomplishments. He'll never know the positive impact he's had on my life and how much of his faith, love, and caring will be passed on to his grandson, and how much better a person my son will be for it. Thank you, Dad.

I want to thank my brother Jeff, for being the brother I always looked up to, and always will. This is very, very hard for me, but I also want to thank my mom Amelia. It's so hard because she passed away five years ago, and I still miss her terribly. She was more like a best friend than a mother, but as a mother, she was everything you'd ever hope a mom would be. She never ever used a computer, but she was a Macintosh person if ever there was one.

Most of all, I want to thank God for the opportunity to be able to write this book; for the work He has done in my life, and continues to do. For always being there when I need Him, and for blessing me with such a wonderful family, and a life I truly love. ■

Foreword

By David Moser (of MacCentral.com fame)

I t was back in 1994 and Web sites supporting the Macintosh platform had just begun to appear on the scene. I had set up a small Mac site called "Mac Toc.com" with the idea of providing Mac users someplace to go online for technical information and help. At around the same time, Stan Flack had launched a Macintosh news site called MacCentral.com (of course, this was long before having dot-com at the end of your name carried a negative connotation).

Just like me, Stan was a one-man show, and struggling to keep up with the enormous task of running a site that was updated daily. I sent him an e-mail offering my assistance, and I suggested maybe we should work together. Before long, I wound up handling sales, marketing, and traffic-building duties for MacCentral.com.

Building visibility for the site was an initial priority, and Stan suggested I contact *Mac Today* magazine, as they had shown support for the site in its infancy. At the time, *Mac Today* was a small magazine, but clearly the most vocal and spirited force in the Macintosh print market. Stan thought that I should contact their editor, Scott Kelby, to see if we could work together to forward our mutual cause—spreading the word about Apple to the Mac faithful.

I "cold-called" Scott at a time when both Macintosh Web sites and Mac magazines were trying to "hold the line," as there was little good news coming out of Apple and it was a tough time to be a Mac user. Within just a few minutes, a relationship was formed, and that one call built the foundation of a partnership that lasts to this day.

Without ever signing a piece of paper (or even meeting face-to-face), our common dedication to the Macintosh platform helped propel MacCentral.com to become arguably the largest independent Mac site on the entire Web, and enabled *Mac Today* to grow into one of the leading Macintosh magazines, outlasting even industry stalwarts like *MacWEEK* and *Mac User*.

Although times have certainly changed since then, and *Mac Today* has evolved into *Mac Design Magazine,* Scott remains one of the most vocal and spirited personalities in the Macintosh arena. That's why I convinced him to write this book. Since Guy Kawasaki's departure from the "Mac space," there just wasn't a beacon in the night for "the rest of us," a "voice of Macintosh" representing the people who care so passionately about the computer, and I knew in my heart that Scott was the right person to carry that torch forward. His sense of humor, coupled with his deep love of the Macintosh platform make for a book that clearly captures the Mac experience and offers a unique and often hilarious view on what it means to be a Mac user today.

He has created a book that truly reflects the excitement and passion of the Macintosh platform, while keeping you in stitches wondering why all those "PC Weenies" still just don't get it!

DAVE MOSER

Not just naked.
Buck naked!

Before we get to the standard "Why I wrote this book" stuff, let's look at something juicier: "Why I used the word 'naked' twice in the headline for this introduction." According to a comprehensive six-year study conducted at Calumet Neahy University, if you can manage to use the word "naked" twice in the same paragraph, the person reading the paragraph will feel uncontrollably compelled to (a) buy whatever it is you're selling, or (b) strip off all their clothes, *then* buy whatever it is you're selling. I don't know how either of those could be a bad thing, so I went with the "double-naked slam dunk." I hope you don't mind my playing these freaky mind games, but this is a really cutthroat business. Now on to more important matters.

Why I wrote this book

This was the book that had to be written. Bill Gates couldn't stop this book from being published. Steve Jobs couldn't stop it. Why? Because they didn't *know* this book was being published. I never told them, or anyone in contact with them. In fact, I didn't tell my publisher, my wife, close friends, my editor, or even the print shop that actually printed the book (they printed the book in total darkness at my request, which made inking the presses all the more challenging). Okay, I confess. Everything from the second sentence on is a total fabrication, but the first sentence, "This was the book that had to be written," is absolutely true. Because if I had not written this book, I would have breached my contract with the publisher, and they'd probably have taken me to court; so in essence "this is the book that *had* to be written."

What's it about?

It's not another look at Apple's history, or an insider's tale of how Steve Jobs fires anything within a 50-yard "blast zone" of his black, long-sleeve turtleneck. That's been done to death. It's not packed with times and dates, eyewitness accounts, and aerial photos of Apple's headquarters taken at night by Microsoft employees wearing greasepaint and "cammo." In fact, this book isn't about Apple at all. It's about you, and what life is *really* like when you're a Macintosh user. Face it, we're stuck in a world completely dominated by PCs (and the inherently evil Microsoft Windows Operating System) and frankly, that's a weird place to be. It's fun, but weird. And annoying. In a weirdly fun, yet annoying, kind of way.

Here's the rub: when you buy a dishwasher, it's just a dishwasher. Whether you buy a Maytag or a Kenmore, it doesn't have a major impact on your social standing or your place in the dishwashing world. However, if you buy a Macintosh, your entire life is going to take a decided change. In short—it's gonna get weird.

Parts of it will be sheer joy, like the moment when you uncover the "secret of Macintosh" and can't believe that you've gone this long living "in the dark." Other parts will be humiliating and depressing, like when you meet someone for the first time at a party, mention that you have a Macintosh, and they look at you as though you had asked, "Have you ever considered the benefits of a Universal Life Insurance policy?"

The highs are many. The lows are many. The manys are many. It's a life of extreme passion for a product that creates a real sense of purpose (evangelizing your incredible discovery), coupled with intense moments of frustration and anger (at Microsoft, at the attitude of smug PC users, at Apple's advertising, at Apple's marketing, at Apple management, and pretty much everything Apple does). You'll laugh. You'll cry. You may be drawn to commit a felony (certainly many have), but there's not a sitting circuit court judge in this country who will find you guilty if it's done in the name of furthering the Macintosh cause (at least as far as I can tell).

How this book came to be

The inspiration for this book actually came from a column I've been writing for more than seven years called "Life in the Mac Lane." (It wasn't one long column that took seven years to write—it appeared in every issue of *Mac Today* magazine, and subsequently

Mac Design Magazine, where it's still published to this day (or at least until somebody catches on).

The reason I wanted to write the "Life in the Mac Lane" column in the first place was to point out the overwhelming media bias against Apple; to show how Macintosh users were attacked, humiliated, and berated daily by PC users; and to have a forum where I could vent my frustration about Apple's world class collection of business, advertising, and marketing blunders that would have put any normal company out of business years ago—which is a testament to how insanely great the Macintosh computer truly is.

The column doesn't pull any punches and neither does this book, so don't hold it too close to your face. (Sorry, I saw an opening and I had to take it.) However, anyone who reads my column could sense my underlying passion for the Macintosh and even for Apple itself. They also feel my utter contempt for Microsoft (but not for the reasons everybody else hates Microsoft, as you'll learn later in the book).

So, is this book like a bunch of "Life in the Mac Lane" columns? Well, in a way yes, but it's actually so much more. First, since it's an entire book, rather than just a single column, I can make a killing. (That's totally untrue, but admit it—it made you pause for a second.) The advantage of a book is that I can finally fully explore and expand on these topics in the way I would have loved to, but never could because of the space constraints of a magazine.

Secondly, I wanted this book to be "print therapy" for anyone trapped in a love-hate relationship with Apple. (We love the computer so much that Apple's existence becomes very, very important to us. Which is why we hate all those "what in the hell are they thinking?" decisions Apple sometimes makes, and why we're often forced to don night-vision goggles and peer over rooftops with high-powered rifles.) This book is also ideal for anyone who is forced to work in "a hostile computing environment" (one where your co-workers are smug, arrogant PC users, with the intellectual makeup of chalk).

Is this book for you?

Are you kidding? This book is so for you, I almost included your name in the title. This book is for you if you've ever planned your family vacation around a visit to Apple's headquarters in Cupertino. This book is for you if you ever slapped the old rainbow-colored Apple logo on the rear window of your car, even though at 55 mph, other motorists might mistake it for a gay-pride rainbow (not that there's anything wrong with that).

This book is for you if you ever chased a PC user with a blunt object, took out your years of pent-up frustration, and then stood over them—one foot on their chest, with a cool breeze blowing through your hair, as crowds of approving Mac enthusiasts chanted your name. (Okay, that last one is more of a fantasy, but if it sounds even remotely like any one of yours, *this book is for you.*) This book is for you if you're generally loose or irresponsible with money. (Do you see where I'm going with this?)

What if you're a PC user?

There's still hope, because this book can be your chance to uncover a world of computing delights that dare not speak its name. This can be your opportunity to discover a computing experience that is the exact opposite of every non-gaming computer experience you've ever had (in other words, a *fun* computing experience). Plus, it's a chance to finally find out why they call PC users just that—"PC users," and why they call Mac users "Mac fanatics"!

Not sure you're ready for all this?

I'm not sure either, but I'm willing to take a chance on you. You seem like a bright kid. Sassy. Brash. You kind of remind me of myself when I was your age (which was 2½ years ago). Besides, if you've read this far, you're clearly not offended by someone who uses the word "naked" twice in one paragraph, and that says a lot about you.

Okay, so you think you're ready

Now I must warn you. When you turn the next page, it's gonna get ugly. It's going to create some disturbing visuals (along the lines of Bill Gates wearing a bicentennial t-back) that may stay with you for a lifetime. But I promise you this: When you're done with this book, you'll have enough Mac ammo to put even the most battle-hardened PC user flat on the floor, cowering in the fetal position, sobbing and babbling incoherently, within 60 seconds or less. That's a special gift I'm willing to share with you. See, I really do care. Now let's kick some PC-using butt.

Life after switching to Macintosh

I've said it a million times: "Using a Macintosh is easy. But being a Mac user isn't." (Okay, maybe not a million times, but certainly a few hundred thousand.) So if being a Mac user is so tough, what's it like being a PC user? I can only imagine that it must be something like having an incredibly high metabolism and being the night manager at a Dunkin' Donuts—everything, everywhere you look, is there for you! For PC users, every peripheral, every mouse, almost every magazine, TV show, or software title is usually just for PC users. On the other hand, for Mac users it's more like being part-time employees at Dunkin' Donuts, and we're on the Atkins Diet—we're surrounded by things we can't have, and the night manager is chowing down right in front of us.

Once you buy a Mac, your life will undergo a major change. It's a good change, an amazing change, and once you've used a Mac for just a few months, I promise you, you'll wonder how in the world Microsoft has been able to dupe otherwise good people into not only using Windows, but thinking it's as good as or (God help them) better than a Mac. So part of the "Naked Truth" about Macintosh is that although using a Macintosh is fun, easy, and incredibly fulfilling (well, as fulfilling as an inanimate object can be), being a Mac user can be frustrating, irritating, and even sometimes embarrassing and humiliating. That's why I feel it's important that you get the straight scoop on what it's like to be a Mac user from the start, what you're going to run into, and how to deal with it.

What you'll run into:

As a Mac user, expect to become somewhat of a social outcast. For example, you'll be at a party, chatting with some people you just met, and when the conversation turns to RAM and high-speed Internet access (it always does, by the way), it's going to come out that you're a Mac user. Oh, you can try to hide it for a while, but they'll break you—believe me, these people can smell fear.

One of their classic tactics is to start asking questions about video cards. As soon as someone brings up video cards and asks which one you like the best—BAM—you're busted. Macs have a great video card built-in, and unless you're doing some high-end Digital Video work, as a Mac user, you'll probably never buy a new video card. On the other hand, PC users apparently hate their video cards and they swap out video cards like we empty the trash—once a week whether it needs it or not.

If they don't catch you on the video card thing, they'll get you with a simple tech question on how to configure a particular driver. They're relentless.

There was one instance back in the spring of '94 where I was able to hide my "Macness" during an entire dinner party, and I would've gotten away with it, too. But I had a little too much to drink that night, and when the host took my car keys, he saw my Apple key chain. I woke up two days later, covered in baby oil and stuffed inside the shipping crate for a Dell 21" monitor near the loading ramp of a Circuit City. Someone had scrawled on the outside of the box, "How do you like your Mac now, Apple boy?" It wasn't pretty.

For a long time, I was certain there was a secret pact among PC users who, when faced with people of questionable computing backgrounds (they sensed a Mac user), would start asking a series of pre-planned questions (no doubt created by a division of Microsoft) that would ferret out any outsiders. Either that or because PC users have such frequent problems, when two or more of them get together they see it as a one-on-one tech support opportunity and immediately begin to probe for possible solutions. Either way, it's creepy when it's happening to you. You can only nod "knowingly" and deftly pass the question to the geek standing to your left for so long, until eventually someone asks you, point-blank, what brand of PC you have. You can either lie or suffer the shame and humiliation that comes with being "the Mac user."

How to deal with it:

I've heard that it's very common for police officers to wind up with other police officers becoming their closest friends. They say the reason for this is that only police officers can truly understand what other police officers are all about, and the challenges and frustrations they face; and this bonds them together. I believe the same concept holds true for Mac users, and that's why it's important to start making some Mac friends—people who share your excitement, challenges, and frustrations as a Mac user in a PC-dominated world. I'm not saying you shouldn't have any PC-using friends (after all, who would there be to tease?), but if you have a few Mac friends, you'll have a support group you can go to after you've had a bad encounter with a PC weenie. They'll basically "delouse" you, briefly share your pain, and get you back on track to your once-happy, well-adjusted life. It's also great to have this core group of Mac buddies to plug-in to social situations (such as seminars, parties, computer store openings, or anywhere that PC users congregate to talk about scintillating topics like tracking down viruses and fixing I/O problems).

There's almost an unspoken bond between Mac users, and when you find one, you have such neat things in common that making Mac friends becomes very easy.

How do you find other Mac users? Here's a hint: Wear Apple stuff and they'll come to you! Go to Apple's Web site (www.apple.com), search for T-shirts, and you'll come across at least a few items of Apple's latest logo-branded wear (plus ball caps and such) that are guaranteed to draw Mac users like cruise ship passengers to the midnight buffet. Also check out www.macsurfshop.com, because they usually have a large selection of Apple-branded items.

Another great place to make Mac friends is at a Macintosh User Group (called MUGs). Most medium-to-large cities already have them (some have more than one), as do many colleges and universities. Again, search Apple's Web site and you'll find a listing of officially recognized groups sorted by city and state.

To this day, I'm still close with a number of people I met in my early days at the local Mac Users Group (including the Editor of this book, Richard Theriault), and besides making friends, it's a great place to do some really quality PC-bashing. Oh, you will find the occasional "can't-we-all-just-get-along, holier-than-thou, about-it-all" Mac user there too, but most of the time, it doesn't take much prodding to get a full-fledged PC bash-fest going. The next thing you know, you're all piling into a minivan on the way to CompUSA for a clandestine operation to bring up Apple's Web site on the Web browser of every computer in the PC section of the store. It's sad, but that's what we do. Oh, after this it's customary to go for a slice of pie to celebrate our small, but symbolically important victory.

Oh yeah, another way to spot potential Mac friends happens right in your own neighborhood. Keep an eye out on garbage day and before you know it, you'll see somebody discarding the shipping carton that their iMac or G4 came in. Stroll by wearing an Apple shirt, and the next thing you know you're both piling into a minivan on your way to CompUSA for a late-night "special op."

What you'll run into:

You go into the local office supply superstore (Staples, Office Depot, etc.), stroll through their computer department, and you don't see anything for the Mac. Not a software package, nary a keyboard, mouse—nothing! It's all PC stuff wall-to-wall.

How to deal with it:

This is one of the realities that you have to come to grips with as a
Mac user because Macintosh software, hardware, and peripherals
are primarily sold through catalog mail order houses ("mail order"
is obviously an outdated term—these days you call their toll-free
number or buy online right from their Web site).

In the Mac market there are a number of huge catalog retailers,
and most of the Mac equipment I've bought during my life I've
purchased this way (as have most of my friends). Honestly, I wish the
office supply superstores carried loads of Macintosh equipment, but
it's just not going to happen, so put it out of your mind and stay
clear of their computing sections—believe me, you'll be happier
for it.

Besides, there are three big advantages to ordering your Mac
stuff through these catalog companies, rather than the office
supply superstores:

(1) They have a huge selection of Mac products, bigger than any
retail store I've ever seen, and most items are in-stock ready to ship.
(2) Mac mail order houses are notoriously competitive with each
other, and just about everything is sold at discount prices, generally
well below the price that your office supply superstore would've sold
the identical products.
(3) Usually, you don't have to pay sales tax when ordering from one
of these catalog companies, so you're going to save right off the top.

The disadvantages are:

(1) It really cuts down on your opportunities to shoplift.

(2) You can't get it today. You can usually get it shipped for delivery the next day (and some Mac mail order houses will let you order as late as 11:00 p.m. and still guarantee delivery the next day), but the soonest you'll get it is the next day.

(3) You may have to pay shipping. I say "may" because sometimes they waive shipping fees (if you order a lot of items), and they often run deals with free or discounted shipping.

Apple also has a very popular online store called (surprisingly enough) the Apple Store, where you can order hardware, but not a lot of software or peripherals—it's mostly Apple's own products. Buying from Apple's Online Store has its own separate set of disadvantages that make it (in my own opinion) a bad choice for mail order purchases:

(1) **You're going to pay sales tax:** Since Apple sells products through stores in all 50 states, Apple has to charge you the sales tax for your state even though you're technically buying online. This negates one of the main advantages of buying online—no sales tax.

(2) **Bad returns policy:** Up until recently, the Apple Store's policy was that once you received your product, as long as it wasn't broken or defective, they didn't take anything back. Period. If you bought from them and you didn't like the product, you couldn't even think about returning it. I've tried, at length, with absolutely no success, and because of that, I've never ordered from the Apple Store again. But Apple has finally eased that policy, and you now have up to 10 days to return the product for a refund (minus a 10% charge if you dared to actually open the shipping carton), but here's the real catch:

Apple won't let you return a custom-configured machine. That may sound reasonable at first glance, but think about it—if you simply add a few megs of RAM when you order it—they've got you—it's a custom machine, and now you can't return it. Bigger hard drive— you're out of luck. Add a Zip drive—and you better like that machine 'cause it ain't going back. Apple touted the ability to custom-configure your Mac as one of the big benefits of ordering from their online store, but if you don't like yours, it can turn into one of its biggest drawbacks.

(3) **You pay full retail price:** Oh, there's occasionally a deal to be found (like they'll throw in some RAM when you buy a new Mac, though most catalog retailers run that deal from time to time), but generally, I've found that the Apple Store has the highest prices on Apple equipment of any retailer on the Web.

So why would *anyone* buy from the Apple Store? Well, there are a couple of reasons why you should (or in some cases, you have to). One of the Apple Online Store's main advantages is that it's often the first, and sometimes the only, place you can get just-introduced Apple products. For example, back when Apple first introduced their SuperDrive (CD-player, DVD player, and CD-writer all-in-one), the only way you could get that particular drive was as a "Build-to-order" from the Apple Store. It was that way for a while, and eventually those drives trickled down to other retailers; but if you were dying to get your hands on one, you had to go to Apple's Online Store.

Another neat thing about the Apple Store is that Apple sells "refurb" units there, and that's the one place on their site where you can find some really great deals. Their prices are generally pretty decent and I haven't heard of anyone (at least, anyone I know) having problems with an Apple refurb they bought online from Apple.

Yet another advantage is specific to people who are concerned about getting ripped off online. If Apple's anything, they're very reputable, so if buying online makes you squeamish, you can be sure Apple's not there to rip you off.

Also, Apple's Online Store is very well designed, neatly organized, and they make it easy to find what you want and buy it. The Apple Online Store phone reps are well trained, friendly (even when telling you that you can't return anything); and they are knowledgeable, so you'll get good info to help with your buying decisions. A lot of people really like Apple's Online Store, some swear by it—I'm just not one of them.

So where can you get your hands on Mac stuff *today?* Generally, in three places:

(1) The Apple Store: Not the online one, the physical one. Apple has opened stores all across the country, mostly in shopping malls, and they're well stocked, well maintained, and staffed by real Apple-trained Macintosh people. The stores themselves kind of remind you of the Gap clothing store—wide open and breezy, with a very consumer-friendly look.

(2) Apple resellers: There are still a number of Apple resellers all over the country, and many of them have really great stores. Some of the better ones I've personally seen are Elite Computers & Software right in Cupertino across the street from Apple's headquarters, but not owned by Apple; MacNet Computer Center in Maui, Hawaii, right near the airport; and DataVision in Manhattan is awfully nice too.

(3) CompUSA: As of this writing, CompUSA still maintains an "Apple Store within a Store" in most of their stores nationwide. (Read the chapter on CompUSA to learn why, although CompUSA sells a decent amount of Mac stuff, going there can become your own personal hell.)

What you'll run into:

There will be a piece of software you want that isn't available for the Mac, and chances are it's a game.

How to deal with it:

This may be the "suckiest" single thing about being a Macintosh user: You are, without a doubt, going to find applications (especially games) that simply aren't available for the Macintosh. It only makes sense, there are more than 10 times as many PC users as there are Mac users, so you can expect that they're going to have at least 10 times more software. When it comes to PC-based games, there are probably 50 times more games. It's frustrating, but that's the way it is.

The only silver lining is that over the years there have been studies of people's computing habits, and one that I found particularly interesting revealed that people generally use just a handful of programs. Even though there are tens of thousands to choose from, in real life people primarily stick to these core applications that they use day in, day out (in other words, they're not running 30 different applications a day, more likely three or four). Over the course of a week, your average user probably uses a Web browser and e-mail application, a word processor, a spreadsheet application, a database, a financial or tax program, and maybe a graphics program or two. So even though PC users have just about a gazillion applications to choose from, they wind up using the same three or four applications most of the time.

You can take some solace in knowing that most of the best-selling business applications on PC are also available for the Mac. Most people are surprised to find out that Microsoft is often the #1 developer of software for the Macintosh platform (shocking, I know). Because of that, you'll have access to Microsoft Office, which includes both Microsoft Word and Microsoft Excel (the most popular spreadsheet application). If you make presentations, just like the PC users, you'll probably use Microsoft PowerPoint; and when it comes to the Web, Microsoft's Internet Explorer Web browser and Outlook Express e-mail client come pre-installed on every Macintosh.

The most popular software for personal and business finance, Quicken, is available for both Mac and PC, and believe it or not, the second most popular database *for the PC*—FileMaker Pro—is made by an Apple spinoff.

As you might expect, all the leading graphics software is available for the Mac, including Adobe Photoshop, QuarkXPress, Macromedia FreeHand, Adobe PageMaker, Adobe Illustrator, Macromedia Director, CorelDRAW, Macromedia Dreamweaver, and just about every graphics app you can think of. (In fact, most of them were available on the Mac first; for example, Photoshop,

QuarkXPress, PageMaker, and Illustrator. More on that later.) So in short—don't sweat the "PC-users-have-all-the-great-applications" thing—the PC programs you're most likely to need will be available for you on the Mac too. But it's those little PC programs that really get to you: Those programs that don't have a big enough audience for the developer to consider making a Macintosh version, but that make you want them even more.

Ah, but there is another solution if you really *need* to run a PC application, but don't want a PC (hey, I don't blame you). It's called Virtual PC (from Connectix). It's an application that lets you run Microsoft Windows and most PC applications right on your Mac. My wife uses Virtual PC at the office, where she uses a PC software program called Policies Now! designed to help create employee manuals and other HR-related documents. It's not available for the Mac, so she bought Virtual PC and now she runs it—right on her iMac. You can switch back and forth between Windows and Mac with just a simple keyboard shortcut, and you can even use the same printer connected to your Mac to print from within Virtual PC. It's amazingly well done, and since it uses a real licensed version of Windows, you get just a taste of just how bad Windows users really have it. If there's anything that makes you glad you use a Mac, it's dabbling in Windows once in a while.

However, when it comes to games, it's a totally different story. I have to be honest—if you're really into the gaming aspect of owning a computer, don't look to the Mac to quench your thirst. Oh sure, some great PC games are now available on the Mac, such as Doom, Tomb Raider, etc.; but really, although the Macintosh does a great job at gaming, there's just not a robust enough collection of games to make it a real *gaming machine* (hey, I told you being a Mac user wouldn't be easy). If you're really into games, honestly, go and buy a Sony PlayStation. Seriously, buy a PlayStation and you'll have more great games to choose from than you ever imagined, and you can buy it for a fraction of the cost of a PC, without any of the hassles and technical support problems that come with trying to maintain and troubleshoot a PC.

But there's yet another way—believe it or not, there is a "PlayStation emulator" (that was also made by Connectix) called Virtual Game Station that lets you play Sony PlayStation games right on your Macintosh (and it's cheap—like $49). My buddy Jim has one, and it works amazingly well for many PlayStation games. When he brings his son Kevin into the office, he'll set him up on an iMac with this emulator running, and when you see him playing Sonic the Hedgehog, you'd swear you were watching a PlayStation. So that's another option if you really want games.

But why are PC users so hooked on gaming? Here's my theory: I've always felt that PC users prefer to play games on their PCs (rather than on a dedicated game machine like a PlayStation or Nintendo) because it somehow justifies buying their PC in the first place. If they play games on their PC, they're technically "using their computer." It's almost like work. They're sitting in their home office, in front of their computer, using the computer; and therefore, in their mind it's somehow "okay." However, if they were just sitting in front of a TV screen with a Sony PlayStation, well…then they'd be just wasting time playing games. It's totally a perception thing, but it's a very strong perception thing (and a key component of Microsoft's plan for world domination). Plus, it's pretty tricky to try to sneak a PlayStation into your office at work without getting caught, but it's easy to install a game on your PC, and when nobody's looking, you're fighting your way out of a cave armed only with your wits and a 20mm cannon.

I have to admit, this lack of access to games sometimes really gets to me. What's weird is—I'm not a big games guy, so I really shouldn't care, but on some level I do. I only own about four games, and only one is installed on my home computer. I probably play that game (Beach Head 2000) about once every two weeks. (Except for the week when I first got it. I played it nonstop for hours on end, until I realized that my wife and son had packed their belongings and moved out. This was incredibly inconvenient, because I had to pause the game, drive all over town searching for them, convince them to come home, and then quickly signal my supply plane before my ammo and health ran out.)

There is one game in particular that's not available for the Mac that really cranks me: Microsoft Flight Simulator. They did make a Mac version years ago, but eventually they stopped (as part of their evil plot) and I really miss it. Sure, the top-of-the-line simulator "Fly" is available on Mac—I just don't care. I want Microsoft Flight Simulator, and it really burns my toast that there's no Mac version. Whew. There. I said it. Now it's off my chest, and I can get back to searching for my supply plane.

What you'll run into:

If you read about Apple in a newspaper or magazine, or see a report about Apple on TV, it's always going to be negative. Always. Even if it's good news, they'll add a negative spin to it. If you see a TV anchor report that Apple posted earnings of $127 million for the quarter, that announcer must, by federal law, add the disclaimer "but they're not out of the woods yet." This "unwritten rule" has been in place for years, and I think it's finally gotten to the point that even if *Apple* issues a press release of any kind, at the bottom of the release where they give a quick explanation of who Apple is by saying "Apple ignited the personal computer revolution," *they* feel they should follow that sentence with "but apparently we're not out of the woods yet" (they don't really add it, but it's certainly implied).

How to deal with it:

It's always, always going to be that way. Why? Because nearly every journalist everywhere uses a PC. These aren't Apple users, who really know Apple, reporting on the company. Instead, reporting on Apple is done almost exclusively by people who chose to use a competing product, reporting on the product they didn't choose. It's like asking a salesman from the local Ford dealership to go on TV and tell America about the new lineup of Chevy trucks. This is just the tip of the iceberg of this subject, and we'll get more into it later in the book, but suffice it to say this is not likely to change, regardless of Apple's situation.

What you'll run into:

You go to the local bookstore, find the Macintosh section, but it's only one or two sets of shelves.

How to deal with it:

There aren't nearly as many books about the Mac OS as there are about Windows, for one simple reason—there's no need for them. The Mac OS is the best designed, easiest to learn, and most fun to use operating system out there. You don't need 200 books as thick as the dictionary to learn how to format a disk. Although the Mac OS is the most powerful operating system, it's not the most complex to use, because it's been designed from the ground up to be easy and accessible. So don't expect shelves and shelves of "How-do-I-uninstall-a-program" books in the Mac area.

Also, until Mac OS X was introduced, most of the Macintosh operating systems were all built on the same foundation, and whether you were using Mac OS 8, 8.1, 8.5, 8.6, 9.0, or 9.1, they all pretty much acted the same (there were some differences, but if you had OS 9.1, and bought an 8.6 book, you'd get 90% of what you need out of that book). But for Windows, all bets are off. There's Windows 95, 98, ME, 2000, XP, and NT, and people are still using all of them daily; and NT and ME are miles apart from each other, so you need loads of books for each (and an engineering degree wouldn't hurt).

Now, here's probably the most important thing about Mac books at the bookstore—the majority of them aren't in the Macintosh section. That's right, books about how the Mac OS works are in the Mac section, but books about Macintosh software are all over the entire computing book section. For example, if you wanted Deke McClelland's excellent Photoshop book *The Macworld Photoshop Bible*, you wouldn't look in the Macintosh section, you'd look in the graphics section. You'll find dozens of books on Photoshop, where every screen capture is taken on the Macintosh version of Photoshop, and every keyboard shortcut includes the Mac keyboard shortcuts. Same thing for other graphics applications like Illustrator

and FreeHand, PageMaker and Quark, or Web-authoring apps like
Dreamweaver and GoLive. They're clearly books written by
Macintosh users, using the Mac version of the software, but they're
not in the Mac section. Same goes with books about graphic design,
multimedia, audio, digital video, or anything creative. Even books
on photography often have a Mac slant because so many professional photographers use Macintosh. Go directly to those sections
and you'll find loads of books that speak the Mac language.

What you'll run into:

All Macintosh people love *Star Trek*. Men, women, it doesn't
matter—they all love at least one or more of the *Star Trek* series
(*Next Generation, Deep Space 9, Enterprise,* etc.).

How to deal with it:

If you really want Mac friends, you'd better pick a series and start
watching reruns now so you can bond on a whole other level.

CHAPTER TWO

"I can't believe you actually use a Macintosh!" and other stupid things PC users say

It was probably five years ago, but I remember it as if it were four years and 11 months ago. My wife and I had become friends with a young couple who lived not far away, despite the fact that the husband was a diehard PC user and he knew I was a total Mac head. Because I knew he was a PC user, anytime the conversation steered toward computing, I took the wheel and veered toward the nearest exit, for the sake of the friendship (okay, for my wife's sake). Every time we'd get together, the husband (to protect his identity, we'll just call him "idiot") would want to talk about computers. He had the whole "I'm an arrogant PC expert" thing going on, so I really didn't want to go there, and I was able to avoid the computing topic completely for quite a while.

One night, we invited the couple over for dinner, and afterward, he and I wound up in my home office talking about software. He was interested in the Web, and I started telling him about a new Web application called Adobe PageMill, which enabled you to build Web pages without having to hand-code HTML. The neat thing was, it was Mac-only, so he had never heard of it, and he was actually interested in seeing it. So I fired up the Mac and launched into my PageMill demo.

I was showing him the various features and how easy it was to build Web pages, and I noticed that as I was demoing the product, he was snickering under his breath. Finally, I guess he just couldn't keep it inside any longer and he took a pot shot at my Mac. Now, up to this point, it had been very cordial. Even fun. We were just two computer buddies looking at a cool new program—the act that has now officially replaced "tossing the football" as a legitimate male-bonding ritual. After which, we should be well on our way to hanging out at the local Home Depot and replacing spark plugs, but he couldn't help himself. He snickered, leaned back in his chair, and with a smirk said, "Hey, when you're ready for a real computer with real speed, you need a PC."

Suddenly a shot rang out, and there he was, lying in a pool of…okay, I didn't shoot him, but I did momentarily consider reaching silently into my desk drawer for the 9mm pistol I keep handy for just such occasions. Even though I didn't brandish a firearm, I could tell he was clearly uneasy (kind of the same uneasiness you might feel if you somehow angered a postal employee).

I gave him my "I now have total disdain for you and everything you stand for" glare and said, "If I really wanted the fastest computer, why in the world would I buy a PC, since the fastest personal computer on earth is a Macintosh?" He scrunched up his nose as if he smelled a dirty diaper and said, "Nah, it's not a Mac…is it?" "Oh yes, my friend, it's a Mac," I replied, "The Power Computing Mac Clone clocks in at 225 MHz, faster than any PC ever made." (Don't forget, this all took place over five years ago, so back then, this *was* the fastest box on the planet. Today a 225-MHz machine is considered so slow you wouldn't use it to design your kid's birthday party invitation.)

He shot back with, "Hey, the Pentium P6 chip is that fast; you just can't buy them yet." So I said, "In other words, some chip in a testing laboratory somewhere is theoretically as fast as a Mac. How does that help *you?*" He cringed a bit after hearing his silly Pentium P6 argument out loud, and retorted, "Yeah, but with a PC, you can buy a case, and all the internal parts, and build a computer for yourself from the ground up. You can't do that with a Mac!"

Now I was thinking to myself, "Oh my God, this guy is assembling a PC in his garage; he's a bigger geek than I thought." I assured him that the last thing a Mac person would ever want to do is sit in their garage and cobble together a computer. If they want a custom Mac, they'll call Power Computing and order one built to their specs (you know, like Apple, Gateway, and Dell do today). Building your own computer is just so "un-Mac-like." We want to *use* our computers, not tinker with them.

Okay, so he blew his PC speed challenge argument, and his "build-your-own-PC" tirade was met with rolling eyes and a general "who gives a flyin' crap," and at this point, I was already starting to figure out how I was going to break the news to my wife that we needed to open a new can of friends. Ah, but he just couldn't leave it alone. He had to add a line that was so out of *The Twilight Zone* that it shot down my spine like a Japanese bullet train. He said, "Yeah, but at least when my PC crashes, I can leave Windows, go into DOS, and fix the problem. When your Mac crashes, you have to send it to the repair shop." I looked at him as if he were trying to tell me "Tobacco isn't addictive," and I asked him, "Where in the Wide World of Sports did you hear that?" He said a friend had told him that this was one of the biggest problems with Macintosh. Because it didn't have DOS (where you could fix crash problems), you had to box up your Mac and ship it to the nearest authorized Apple repair center, where they would "un-crash it" and then send it back to you. I just laughed and shook my head.

I showed him how we force-quit a program to recover from a crash using just a keyboard shortcut, or how we can reboot and the Mac is up and running again. He seemed genuinely intrigued, so I took the opportunity to show off more of the Mac's features, including the built-in ability to read, write, and format PC disks as well as Mac disks. He said, "Oh yeah, my PC can do that, too." So I said, "You mean to tell me you can get in your car right now, drive to your house, and pop this Mac disk in your floppy drive, and it will read my Mac files?" He said, "Well…no."

See, that's the crap I'm talking about. They're so reluctant to admit that anything on a Mac is better than their PC, that they'll lie to cover it up. Now, are there programs today that you can buy to read Mac disks on a PC? Absolutely. So what's the catch? They're extra programs that you have to buy—they ain't cheap—and you have to install them, and then learn how to use them, just to get a feature that comes standard on every Macintosh.

Then I showed him the Mac's built-in Find function, for finding files on the drive, and he said, "Windows has a built-in find function too, it just doesn't have as many options." I said, "Oh, you mean it's not as *powerful* as the Mac's find function?" At this point, I could tell he just wanted to be out of there, because his finely crafted PC defense mechanism had failed him miserably, and he realized that pretty much everything he thought he knew about the Mac was completely and utterly wrong.

The bad thing about it is, my ex-friend is not unique. In fact, he's the norm. He's a typical Mac-basher. He takes shots at the Mac, uses his status as a self-proclaimed "PC expert" to advise people strongly against buying a Mac, yet he thinks that if your Mac crashes, you send it back to the factory. This supports my theory that PC experts (geeks who can assemble a box of crap in their garage) know the least about Macintosh of anyone on the planet. So where did this "PC expert" gain his cumulative knowledge about the Macintosh? From a PC-using friend who obviously knows less about the Mac than he does (if that's even possible).

I guess the worst part of this story is that this total ignorance, coupled with a lack of respect based on that ignorance, has formed the basis of how Mac users are perceived and treated by many PC users. We have a name to describe people who fit into this Mac-bashing category: "PC Weenies." Now mind you, not everyone who uses a PC is a PC Weenie—this is a particular psychological profile of people who (a) don't really know anything about the Mac, and (b) attack what they don't understand, or whatever Microsoft tells them they should attack. We also call them "PC Losers, Goobers, or just plain PC Idiots," but the Weenies term has really taken on a life of its own, so I'll use it liberally from here on out.

He's not alone; they come in packs

I had another major "weenie" encounter (I know that sounds like a line from a torrid romance novel, but it's not meant to) a few years ago, after my wife and I moved into a cozy little neighborhood not far from our office. A neighbor was walking his dog, the dog got loose, wound up in my yard, and after the man retrieved his pooch, he introduced himself, and we started the neighborly chat thing.

He had a computer-related job of some sort (probably a network administrator or PC consultant. I really don't remember), but we were having a nice "get-to-know-your-neighbor" chat when he asked me what I did for a living. I told him, "I'm the editor of a computer magazine…" and as those words were rolling off my tongue, I could see his eyes widen in anticipation as he broke into a huge grin. I could tell he was thinking, "Oh God, let this be the editor of *PC Computing* or *PC Magazine.* We'll be the best of friends, and I'll get VIP passes to computer events, and he'll get me all kinds of freebies and software. Imagine that: Me—best buddies with the editor of a computer magazine. I hit the jackpot!" and then I finished my sentence with "…for Macintosh users." I swear it was if someone had slugged him in the stomach. His grin instantly disappeared and was replaced by a look of utter disappointment bordering on total disgust. Honestly, within about 20 seconds, our "neighborly chat" was over, and he quickly walked back to his house. That was more than three years ago, and to this day he's never spoken to me again. My wife told me that a few months back he had moved away. What a shame.

Skip the bonding

In this case of the PC-loser neighbor, he didn't really say anything stupid—he didn't have to. Had I been an editor for *PC Magazine*, we'd have probably gone straight into the garage and started assembling a beige box of wires as a first step on our path to lifelong friendship. Instead, he retreated to his house where I'm certain he cowered in a dark corner quietly sobbing for hours (at least, that's what I was hoping). His face and actions did the talking for him, but I'm normally not that lucky. Usually, the PC users will attack me head on, as soon as they learn that I use a Mac.

Life on the street

I remember a few years back going to a local computer store to buy a Gravis GamePad (it's a cross between a joystick and a PlayStation controller, and it's very popular on the Mac). I went to the gaming section of the store, and I looked around a bit but couldn't find it. Finally, in desperation I asked the salesperson if he could help me find the GamePad (incidentally, asking a salesman in a computer store for Mac software or hardware is technically considered "desperation" and is used only as a last resort). The salesperson looked at me as if I was speaking a foreign language. I repeated, "The Gravis GamePad?" He looked irritated and muttered, "I don't think we have one," and he feigned trying to look for one for about 15 seconds.

Another shopper was standing near the salesman and pointed out a Gravis GamePad to him, so the salesman turned and blankly handed me the GamePad from the shelf. I looked at the box, and then asked him, "Do you have the Macintosh version?" There was a brief pause, and then both the once-helpful customer and the generally disinterested salesman simultaneously broke out in laughter (at this point, my wife took two steps back to avoid the shock wave from the impending blast).

As my blood pressure crept higher, the salesman (suddenly alive and animated) continued with a chuckle, "They don't make much hardware for Macs." (They both giggled.) I grabbed a shrink-wrapped box of Microsoft Excel from a nearby shelf and started beating both of them repeatedly with the 9-pound software package-turned-weapon, until they were within an inch of their lives (that's not what really happened, but boy would it sell some books if it had).

What really happened was that my wife grabbed my arm with her "Honey, let them live" grip and started leading me toward the door. But just as I was turning to leave, as if the hand of God had come down and placed it there, I saw a Gravis GamePad for Macintosh on a lower shelf. I pulled it from the shelf, stuck it right in the salesman's face, and said, "It's right here, see…Macintosh version!"

He said, "Gee, I'm surprised. Only about 2% of our business is Macintosh. People come in here all the time and ask for Mac stuff, but only the first two shelves are for Mac." I looked at him like the condescending PC bonehead that he was and asked, "If people come in all the time asking for Macintosh software, wouldn't it make sense to carry more?" He just looked at me blankly again and shrugged. When people wonder why I'm so defensive about Macintosh, this is the kind of stuff I'm talking about.

Where's Emily Post when you need her?

Here's what really bothers me: This kind of treatment is a breakdown of some social order and shows a total lack of simple manners and common courtesy. I mean, who raised these people, Bill Gates?

For example, if you were at a party and you met a person who told you they just bought a new Audi Quattro, you wouldn't say, "Oh man, I can't believe you bought an Audi. Are they even still in business? That's not a car—it's a joke. You should get a real car, like my Dodge Intrepid." Of course, you'd never say that because it's rude and inappropriate, especially toward someone you just met. Besides showing a total lack of simple, common courtesy, it's just plain mean and certainly not a good way to make friends. Plus, really, if they bought an Audi (which, as a company, makes some really great cars), why would you care? Their purchase of an Audi doesn't affect your life as a Dodge owner in any way, shape, or form. It's a nonevent.

More likely, your response to learning that someone you just met bought a new Audi would be, "Hey that's great. How do you like it?" Simple. Polite. Pretty much a pleasant "small-talk" type of comment. But here I am in a computer store, speaking to a salesperson who's there (ostensibly) to help me, and standing nearby is a customer who's not being addressed by me or the salesperson, and within seconds of finding out that I own a Macintosh, both are literally laughing in my face. It's just plain rude.

Now, I know that if you met either of these two people outside the computer store, in virtually any social situation, and you told them you bought an Audi, both of them would be polite and courteous about your choice of automobile. But if you follow that up by divulging that you own a Macintosh, all bets are off—they load their cannons and tell you what an absolute idiot you are for not buying what they bought. How does it impact their lives if you choose a different operating system than they do? Why should they even care? This "bash the Mac user" scenario plays out again and again, every day, all over the world—I know because I've lived it hundreds of times, and still run into it today.

Mac classic

Here's a classic case: A few years back, we had outgrown our office space and were looking for a new location. We found some suitable offices in a building on the same street as our existing location, and one day I took a couple of guys from work down to see what would soon be our new digs.

As we were looking around, one of the other tenants came by and introduced himself. He told us he was an accountant, and he asked us what line of work we were in. We told him that we published a Macintosh magazine. It was almost like someone uncorked his "stupid valve" and out came pouring a collection of thoughtless rude comments that only a true PC Weenie can make.

His first comment was "Isn't Apple going out of business?" Now, imagine meeting someone for the first time, they tell you where they work, and you immediately insult them by asking, "Hey, isn't your company going out of business?" How incredibly rude! That's a sure-fire recipe to get the person you just met to hate you. Back to our story: We had to interrupt and let him know that Apple had just posted a $47 million dollar profit, and that it was their third profitable quarter in a row, while other PC manufacturers were struggling to survive.

Of course, in true weenie fashion, he clearly didn't believe
that Apple was posting profits, and he went on to argue the point
that it couldn't be true, because none of his other friends in the
"accounting field" used Macs. Well, duh! What a shock—none
of his friends in accounting used Macs. In fact, he said he didn't
know anyone who uses a Macintosh (and believe me, after talking
to him for two minutes, it was absolutely certain that he didn't know
anyone with a Macintosh, because I can't imagine a Macintosh user
who would tolerate him). He went on and on, digging himself
deeper and deeper into a hole, until he could tell that he had angered
us to the point that even though we hadn't yet moved in, we were
certainly not looking forward to it.

When I talk about Mac-bashing, this is exactly what I mean.
When he told me he was an accountant, maybe I should have said,
"Accountant? Aren't computing programs like QuickBooks going to
do away with the need for accountants? Besides, what a boring job,
and seriously, how many tax returns can you really do within a year.
Isn't that kind of limiting? I bet you're a big hit at parties, being an
accountant, and all, etc." That's pretty much the equivalent of what
he said to us. He basically said, "The company that you've based your
business on is going out of business, nobody uses the computer
you're supporting, and you guys are idiots."

Luckily, within a few years we outgrew that office (Apple miracu-
lously had *still* not gone out of business), and we moved to an even
bigger space in a nearby city. We really missed him.

A shining glimmer of hope

My brother has a pretty decent theory on why he believes that God must really like golf (and my brother isn't exactly what you'd call a deeply religious man, so anytime he comes up with a theory involving God, it's worth a listen). He says, "You know how some days you're out on the course, and you're just having one of the those days where you can't hit anything but water, sand, and nearby houses. You're throwing your clubs, cussing like a sailor, and you're about ready to give up the game, but then out of nowhere, God lets you hit a perfect shot—one glorious shot that's straight down the fairway, long, high (but not too high), and after a nice bounce it rolls right up on the green (where you're guaranteed to 3-putt), and you stand back and think, 'Hey, now *that* was pretty. I guess I can still play after all,' and that one perfect shot is what keeps you from throwing your clubs in the water and giving up the game for life."

I have a similar theory about God and the Macintosh. I've always felt pretty certain that if God uses a computer, it's definitely a Mac. (After all, since money is no object to Him, and He can choose the best computer in the world, why would He choose a PC, which is clearly the devil's work?)

Since God likes the Mac, every once in a while he lets you garner a minor victory to keep you on the platform (we're not going to win the war, so we just engage in guerrilla attacks—one PC user at time). But I had one particular win that literally changed my life, *and* the life of the PC Weenie, in a very dramatic way.

It was a dark and stormy night (hey, I said it was dramatic) back in the late '80s, when I was working as a financial consultant (glorified stockbroker) at a large bank. The operations manager was a woman, and her husband would phone to chat with her every day, sometimes several times a day (on company time, mind you).

We had one incoming line, so I'd often happen to take his call, and then put him on hold while I beeped his wife (that's not meant to sound nasty, but after rereading it, it does, and most authors would change that sentence to keep from offending anyone). Anyway, if his wife was busy for a minute, or if she was tied up on another line, we'd wind up chatting; and I guess at some point his wife mentioned to him that I was a Macintosh user—and that was all he needed. If I picked up his call, he would go through the standard Mac attacks of the day, "Macs are toys. Macs are only good for games. Macs aren't real computers, etc." Mind you, this guy was using a DOS machine at work, and seemed to be damn proud of it, but at least he wasn't militant about his remarks. It was more good-natured ribbing than the mean-spirited attacks Mac users usually endure, so I let him live.

We became pretty chummy over the course of the next six months and then we had a brief affair (kidding, totally kidding: it's getting near the end of the chapter and I just wanted to make sure you were still paying attention). Since I was a stockbroker, I closely followed Apple stock, which meant keeping a close eye on Apple news. If Apple landed a big contract, I'd be sure to tease my DOS buddy mercilessly when he'd call. I'd say, "Hey, did you see where Boeing just bought 12,000 Macs? Gee, I wonder what they're doing out there in Seattle with all those Macs. Playing games?", or maybe I'd say, "Wow! Delta Airlines just placed another huge order with Apple. I wonder if they ordered joysticks, too," etc.

I kept chipping away and chipping away at him, until finally one day I could tell he was starting to show signs of weakness and the early-warning signs of what we refer to as an "open mind," so I said, "Hey, one night when you've got nothing to do, why don't you come over to my house and I'll show you my Mac?" (again, it sounds nasty, but it just doesn't bother me enough to change it).

A few weeks later he took me up on the offer, and he came over to my house for the "Macintosh experience." When we were ready to play "computers," I pulled one of the oldest Mac tricks in the book—instead of showing him how my Mac works, I put him in the driver's seat from the very beginning—I let him sit at the Mac and do everything from formatting a disc to deleting a file, and just about everything in between.

It was amazing to see his reaction at finally sitting at a Mac. He was blown away, and I could tell he was genuinely excited about it. Even though he actually liked DOS, and had used Windows pretty extensively, apparently all the things he'd heard about the Macintosh (from his PC-using friends) were wrong, and the Mac totally rocked. So much so, that within a few weeks he bought his first Mac for his home. Then one for the office. Then it wasn't long before he bought one for his wife, his mother, his brother, and eventually for his son. But his dedication to the Mac platform was more than just buying a few computers.

This "DOS buddy" I keep referring to is actually Jim Workman, who cofounded *Mac Today* magazine with me back in 1993, and he's still my friend and business partner (and avid Mac fanatic) to this very day. His wife, Jean, the operations manager for the brokerage firm I worked at, quit her brokerage job about six years ago to come on as our business manager. Score one for the home team.

CHAPTER THREE

Things Apple doesn't tell you about owning a Macintosh

I f Apple told the public all the negative things about owning a Macintosh, it's entirely possible that it might scare you off. That would be terrible, because the great things about owning a Mac tremendously outweigh the few negatives. But you can certainly understand Apple's position. It's the same for the manufacturer of almost any product—saying negative things about your own product just isn't good for sales. It's probably why you don't hear tire companies saying stuff like, "If you're going 80 miles per hour, and one of these babies blows, you're on your way to the morgue." It's just not appealing to consumers, even if it's the truth. In fact, I think consumers must enjoy being lied to or Microsoft would have been out of business years ago (note to Microsoft's lawyers: That was a joke. Just kidding, etc.).

So since Apple's not going to tell you, well…somebody should. Luckily, the stuff I'm going to share is not really bad stuff (after all, this is Apple, not Microsoft), but it's stuff that if you know going in, makes it easier to take later on when it you live it.

What Apple doesn't tell you about *your purchase:*

Shortly after you buy your Mac, not only is the price of the model you just bought going to drop, but Apple is going to either:

(a) increase the speed

(b) add more RAM

(c) add a bigger hard drive, or more likely…

(d) do all of the above.

How often does this happen? Almost always. Why does Apple do this? Are they out to get you, their loyal customer? Absolutely not. They do it to stay competitive. If they don't keep offering faster and faster machines, at better prices, with more features, there won't be an Apple very long. It's an industry based on more; faster; cheaper.

If you're an early adopter (a person who buys the hot new toys as soon as they're announced), there's a price to pay—you get the cool toy first, but a faster, cheaper, better version is already in the works. Look at the people who bought the 20th Anniversary Macintosh introduced in the spring of 1997 for $10,000. Once the initial rush died down, and the early adopters all got theirs, Apple started blowing them out for as low as $1,999, 20% of their original price. Look at it from Apple's position. Let's say they made 12,000 units (according to Apple back in '97 this was how many units they were going to produce), and they sold 9,000 (I'm just picking this number out of the sky, so don't hold me to it, but whatever it was, it was probably less than they perhaps projected) at the $10,000 price. It's maybe 11 or 12 months later (remember, technology years are like dog years—11 months in the tech world is like nearly six years in real life) and Apple is stuck with a warehouse full of 3,000 computers that aren't selling. Worse yet, they're no longer "state-of-the-art" because since they introduced that model, newer models with faster chips and bigger drives are selling like hotcakes. Basically, the window of opportunity for that model has passed. But they've got 3,000 of them sitting in sealed boxes, ready to ship. Do they go back to those old models, rip open 3,000 boxes, open the cases to throw away the old chips, install new chips, and update any other parts (fans, etc.) that might need updating because of the new chip? Or, do they just "blow them out" at a discounted price because they already pretty much made their money back, thanks to the "early adopters?" It's not hard to see why Apple might choose to blow them out. Especially since Wall Street loves to jump on Apple if they have more than just a few days' worth of inventory on hand. (Apple had let inventory stack up pretty seriously on a number of occasions, reportedly as much as 11 weeks or more at one time, so the Wall Street analysts have kept a close eye on it ever since.)

So if you've been stung by the "better, faster, cheaper" bug, don't let it freak you out. The computer you originally bought is still a great computer. When you bought it, you got it at a great price, and it still does exactly what you bought it for. Besides, if you could return it to Apple for what you paid for it, in just a few months the new computer you would buy would meet the same fate as the one you returned. It's a never-ending cycle, so you might as well be happy with the one you bought, because a better, faster, and cheaper model is always "coming soon."

Here's a tip: If Apple suddenly slashes the price on a model, you can figure you've got between 30 and 60 days before it gets upgraded at a lower price. If you're cool with that—you're going to get a great deal (at least you'll feel like it is, for between 30 and 60 days).

What Apple doesn't tell you after *you've bought your Mac:*

Here's the thing: Once you've bought your Mac, you're basically on your own to learn how to use it. Now, Apple does have an owner's manual that is better than most and some tutorials that come with your Mac that can help you get the basics, but beyond that, it's up to you.

Luckily, there are Macintosh User Groups (like I mentioned earlier), but Apple doesn't do a whole lot for them, either. Just ask any user group president how much support Apple gives them. They'll tell you it ranges somewhere between zip and nil.

I've always felt that being a part of a Mac User Group (MUG), and having access to the help these user groups offer their members, is one of the best things about being a Mac user. Having MUGs helps Apple for a number of reasons: These groups educate thousands and thousands of Mac users every month all around the world. They offer training and one-on-one help that is virtually unavailable anywhere else (at least without paying a bundle). When you join a

MUG, you become part of a community where you can get help and support and learn about areas of the Mac you never knew existed.

These MUGs help Apple by evangelizing their products and showcasing Macintosh hardware and software. MUGs help sell more Macs, because simply by being there, they provide support for people who are thinking of buying a Mac—they know they have a place to go to get help. This community makes prospective buyers feel more at ease about buying a product that is clearly not in the majority in computing.

For these reasons, and a dozen more, you'd think that Apple would be throwing tons of money, time, and resources at user groups, but instead they all but ignore them (outside of the occasional visit to some MUGs by a local Apple representative to demo new Apple products).

If the person who runs the User Group Relations program at Apple (and I pray that such a person exists) were to read this, and wrote me a nasty-gram telling me how much they do for MUGs, all I could tell them is, "I know you think you're doing a lot, but trust me—you're not."

Could you imagine how thrilled a company like Trane would be if each month, all around the world, groups of people who have Trane air-conditioning units would gather to help each other learn more about Trane compressors, blowers, and fans, and evangelize other Trane products? Trane would gladly pay millions to have a community like that, because that type of worldwide community is absolutely priceless (for everything else, there's MasterCard—I know, that's a bad one).

What Apple doesn't tell you about *discontinuing models:*

There's also a reasonable chance that Apple will discontinue your particular model immediately after you buy it. (In fact, I think Apple is secretly waiting for you to buy it, and when you do, an e-mail is automatically generated informing Apple's product team, so they immediately get the wheels in motion to discontinue the product. At least, that's what it feels like.)

It's the same feeling I get after buying stock. I feel that as soon as I place my order with my broker, a secret "sell" code is inserted into the NYSE ticker tape. A secret code that only floor traders know, and it tells them, "Kelby's in, it's time to sell," and they race to unload the stock I bought, in what can only be compared to the final scene from the movie *Trading Places*. If you got a good deal on a Cube, a purple or green iBook, or a G3 tower, you know what I mean.

Another good example is Apple's very cool-looking 17" Studio Display. One day, it was just gone, and Apple no longer offers any displays with a tube—now they're all LCD flat panels. The problem is, the day before Apple announced this, people bought those 17" Studio Displays. It doesn't make them bad displays, it doesn't somehow disable them, but it does make you wonder if you made a mistake.

Again, this possibility of discontinuation doesn't mean that you got a raw deal, or you bought a bad machine, I just want you to know that it could (and does) happen.

What Apple doesn't tell you about *rumors:*

It used to be you could find out just about everything about soon-to-be introduced Apple products on the Web weeks before Apple announced it. You could find prices, specs, complete descriptions, and sometimes even photos online, courtesy of internal leaks at Apple. That was before Steve put the hammer to a few of those leaks and made their level of product secrecy something the CIA could only aspire to. Couple that with a legion of Apple lawyers threatening action on anything that moves, and suddenly, the rumors have come to a halt.

Today, nearly everything you read about an upcoming Apple product is way off base, thanks in part to an Apple disinformation campaign that would make UN weapons inspectors blush. Take the introduction of Apple's iPod. The day before the announcement, an Apple rumor site had posted "sneak peek" color photos of the unit, including full specs, the product name, pricing, and more. It was all completely wrong. The photo was so far off from what Apple announced, it made you wonder if Apple hadn't created the product shot solely to throw the rumor sites off the trail. In short, Apple gives out lots of info, but wait for their official announcement before making the jump.

What Apple doesn't tell you about *transferring files:*

It's much easier to get stuff into your Mac than it is to get stuff out. So if you want to get documents, images, or video clips out of your Mac, you'd better plan to buy something extra to make this possible.

This problem started way back when Apple introduced the first iMac. They made a bold, industry-changing decision to do away with the built-in floppy drive that had been in every Macintosh (and every PC) for more than 10 years. Apple had the right idea: The floppy was a dinosaur—incredibly slow, often unreliable, and the amount of data it could hold was, in this day and age, a joke.

So the decision to do away with the floppy drive may have been right; but the problem is in how Apple replaced the floppy drive—with nothing.

Every Mac comes with a CD-ROM drive of some sort, so getting things into your Mac isn't a problem, but if you're not connected to a network or don't want to (or can't, because of file size) e-mail your file to someone, you're essentially stuck. That document is trapped inside your iMac unless you buy a separate writable drive of some sort.

The frustration of this limitation really hit me one day when we were having an open house at our office. We set up an iMac in the lobby and were going to run a full-screen slide show, featuring covers of the magazine, as the guests arrived. I designed the slide show on my G4, and the entire slide show was only about 320 K in size (less than ⅓ of a MB). So I copied the file onto a 100-MB Zip disk (using my G4's internal Zip drive) and walked over to the iMac in the lobby (this technology of physically walking a file from one machine to another is known as "sneaker net").

When I got there, I realized the iMac didn't have a Zip drive attached (Apple doesn't offer an internal Zip for the iMac, so you'd have to buy an external). So there I was, a half hour before the party, standing there with my tiny 320-K file on a Zip, and I couldn't get it into the iMac. There wasn't a network input in the lobby, so I couldn't connect the iMac to the network, and there wasn't a tele-phone jack there, so I couldn't e-mail it to the iMac. So I went into the graphics department to use a G4 that had a CD-ROM burner connected to it, but sure enough—it didn't have a Zip drive hooked up to it either, so I couldn't get my files into it to burn a CD to transfer the file to the iMac.

I won't bore you with the rest of the calamity, but suffice it to say, it took up until party time to get that stinkin' 320-K file (which would have easily fit on a floppy) onto the iMac. This isn't a plea for Apple to return to the floppy—again, I just wish they had replaced the floppy with something else that would become standard on every Mac (like the floppy was). The CD-ROM burners Apple is now including with some models are great, if you don't mind waiting six minutes while you burn a CD that will wind up holding only 320 K of data.

My point is—what Apple doesn't tell you is—getting files out of your Mac is up to you (through your network, via your e-mail, or via the extra drive you need to buy).

What Apple doesn't tell you about *nonstandard connectors:*

One thing Apple dearly loves to do is change connectors on Mac products. They must love this, because they seem to do it as a regular practice. For example, Apple introduced a monitor that I dearly loved—the 17" Studio Display that I mentioned earlier. The back of the monitor had a clear plastic shell, and you could see all the components inside. It was just so slick. I thought it was the best-looking, best-designed monitor Apple had ever made.

Well, I had been using a Radius PrecisionView monitor for a number of years, and although it was a great monitor, it was "big and beige." The big-and-beige era had long since passed, and now this huge clunky monitor, sitting next to my sleek G4, just looked out of place. So naturally, I wanted one of those cool, new Apple 17" displays. Unfortunately, even though I had a G4, I couldn't use that monitor because Apple created a special connector called the Apple Display Connector (ADC) for it that enabled the monitor to do without a power cord. Instead it would draw its power directly from the USB connector, and this would make your desk area less cluttered. Supposedly this would be especially attractive to Cube owners because they were buying the Cube as a "showpiece" on their "executive desks" (at least, that's the market Apple was supposedly targeting). So, this new connector could only be used by either the Cube (which I didn't have), or a newer G4 than the model that I had. So I was stuck with a big, clunky beige monitor again. Not only was this incredibly frustrating, Apple lost out on a sale of that monitor, which was apparently needed, because they didn't sell enough to keep making them. The nonstandard connector came back to bite them.

It gets worse (for me anyway). At that time, we had a Cube at one of our design stations at the office, and the designer using it wasn't thrilled with its speed; so we bought him a newer, faster machine with all the bells and whistles. Well, I thought I might snag his Cube for my home office, because my home office is right near the master bedroom and the fan on my G4 keeps my wife awake (she has this "superman hearing" thing going on—she can hear things like paint drying, a leaf falling in the park not far from our house, dust settling on the floor, things like that). Anyway, I wanted to connect this Cube to an older Apple 15" flat-panel monitor. Sounds simple, right? Wrong! The connector on the flat-panel won't work with the Cube. Arrgggghh!

It happened again to me just this week, with something so simple. I wanted to do some QuickTime video editing, and I needed to add a voice-over, so I bought an Altec Lansing headset mic. I came home, plugged the mic into the mic input, put the headphones into the audio out, and then I spent the next hour trying to figure out why I could hear the audio perfectly, but the mic didn't work at all. So, at 8:40 p.m., I jumped in the car, headed back down to Best Buy, and returned the Altec Lansing headset, telling the person at the Customer Service desk that the mic was broken. Instead of tempting fate, I bought a Labtec this time. Went home and tried again. Still no mic (so I realized, it wasn't the mic, it was my Mac).

The next day, my neighbor came over and I told him about the problem. We tried his headset mic but it still didn't work, so I figured my audio jack was out. Tried it at work—still no luck. I came to find out that Macs need a special connector (they got me again), and I hate to admit it, but the only thing I could find that had the right connector was a headset mic from (get this) the Macintosh version of IBM's ViaVoice speech recognition package. That's right, I had to use an IBM product to get a mic to work on my Mac. This can only be explained as the PC world getting back at me.

Now I'm sure that I could have done some research and probably found a Mac headset mic somewhere, but as luck would have it, IBM had sent our magazine a copy of ViaVoice for review, and it wound up saving the day.

What really bothers me is, I have a feeling that more nonstandard connectors are on the way because someone at Apple must secretly enjoy them. I know that some of the things I have, use, and enjoy today will not connect to a Mac I'll buy in the very near future (or a new product won't connect to my old equipment). How can this be a good thing? I know some people will argue the point that sometimes there are adapters that will let you use some of these nonstandard connectors with older Macs, but the problem is (a) these adapters aren't always available, and when they do become available, it's always quite a while after the product has been introduced; (b) they're usually from a third party, rather than from Apple; (c) they're expensive; and (d) because they're in huge demand, it seems that they're either out of stock or back-ordered at least three weeks when you really need one TODAY!

So why does Apple keep introducing nonstandard connectors? The next time I'm in a high-level meeting with Apple's management team, you can be sure this "nonstandard connector" issue is one of the topics I'll bring up. (For the record, I've *never* been in a high-level meeting with Apple's management team, and I can't imagine a situation where I would be. Especially after writing this chapter.)

What Apple doesn't tell you about *your love life:*

I hate to be the one to tell you this, but your love life is going to suffer. Remember how Saturday mornings used to be your special time? You'd wake up, spend the morning in bed, reading each other the funnies, giggling, and sharing your innermost secrets? Buy a Mac and those days are gone forever.

Now you're spending Saturday mornings in line waiting for the opening of your local Apple Store. Sunday nights, you're helping your friend who just bought an iMac get connected to the Internet. Friday night you're at CompUSA looking for an adapter to make your new monitor work because you found out the connectors don't match.

Remember how you used to call your mate at work, just to tell her you loved her? Now you call asking her which key you hold down to keep the extensions from loading at start-up. Before you know it, you're both on the Jerry Springer show for a segment called "Macs, and the Women Who Love Them" after you uncover the fact that she secretly bought an iBook and hid it in the pantry for six months without your knowing. There you are, openly sobbing on national TV, when suddenly you're hit by a folding chair, and when you look up, clutching your wife's iBook is the woman who is president of your local Mac User Group. Just before you black out, you hear someone from the audience yell "You go, girl!"

Sadly, the Mac can turn your relationship into a twisted love triangle, and I've seen it tear more than one marriage apart (I haven't really, but I wanted to end with something tawdry enough that it might carry over into the next chapter. Hey, it's worth a shot).

CHAPTER FOUR

The definitive platform test

O ver the years, one thing I feel pretty certain about is that certain people are drawn to certain computing platforms for a reason. Mac and PC users seem to have their own separate sets of personality traits and obviously these have an effect on their decision of which platform is right for them. Otherwise, everybody would be on the same platform (and what a boring world that would be—with everyone using Macs).

This is going to sound a bit judgmental (and if you've read this far, I guess I don't really have to warn you about that, do I?), but many times I can tell who's a PC user and who's a Mac user just by taking a quick look at them.

Here's an example: I've been conducting software training seminars since back in the early '90s. Back then, CD-ROM drives weren't as prevalent as they are today, so we would give the attendees a floppy disk with support files from the seminars (stuff like shareware plug-ins, royalty-free images, etc.) when they picked up their workbook materials in the morning. Well, because the discs were floppies, we had to have separate Mac- and PC-formatted floppies. This necessitated asking each seminar attendee, "Are you Mac or PC?" so we could hand them the right disk for their computer.

It was during this act of handing out floppy disks that I first became aware of the visual differences (hair, clothing, attitude) between Mac and PC users. As a seminar attendee was leaving the registration table and making his/her way toward the materials table, we'd make a call as to whether we thought they'd tell us they were Mac or PC.

Professional odds-makers would love to have our percentages, because right out of the gate we were picking nine out of ten correctly.

Basically, if the person walking toward us looked "cool," they were almost definitely a Mac user. By cool, I mean they dressed casually (maybe in shorts, or a T-shirt), but in general they gave out a cool vibe. Smiling, casual, confident—they looked comfortable in their own skin, and resembled somebody you'd like to hang out with.

On the other hand, it was a dead giveaway that it was a PC user if the person wore a suit, a Polo shirt, and khakis, or if they dressed as they would for the office. If they were uptight during registration or gave the registration staff a hard time, that was another clue. This isn't to say that all PC people are uptight, but if *you* had to deal with countless tech problems while trying to be productive in an environment where your computer is constantly crashing and being invaded by destructive viruses at the same time, it could make you a bit…well…tense. If we spotted a geek, spaz, or dweeb (someone wearing a pocket protector, taped-up horn-rimmed glasses, or if they had "high waters"), we didn't even ask—we just handed them a PC disk. Say what you will, it was amazing how many times we were right.

Another interesting thing was how people responded when we asked them, "Mac or PC?" PC people would just say, "PC," and put out a hand for the disk. No change of expression, no inflection, just "PC." But in this environment (a graphics seminar) when you asked a Mac person, "Mac or PC?" they looked at you as if to say, "Are you kidding? Are there any PC people even here? This is a graphics seminar?" They'd proudly proclaim, "Macintosh!" They'd sometimes add their own custom tweaks to their response. Stuff like "Mac, baby!" or "Mac. Is there anything else?" or my favorite "Mac. Come on, do I look like a PC user?" Even they knew there was a difference.

Why in this situation did the Mac crowd suddenly get so cocky? Because they knew this was the one situation where they would clearly be in the majority. That's why we start each seminar by asking for a show of hands for how many Macintosh people there are in the crowd (we don't ask for Mac users, we ask for Macintosh *people*). When we ask, it seems as if nearly every hand in the room goes up; and most of the time, when the attendees realize that the majority of the people in the room—at a computer seminar—are Mac people, they burst into spontaneous applause and cheers. You see attendees all around the room high-fiving. Honestly, it sounds silly, but it's a beautiful thing to see.

This early visualization of how differently Mac and PC people dress and act helped me develop a sure-fire written test for determining whether you're on the right platform for your personality. This is to be used when a visual determination is unavailable.

I developed this test for a reason. As much as I hate to say it, there are people on the Macintosh platform that really don't belong here. Luckily, it's a very small number. One telltale sign is to drop over to their house unexpectedly and, when they invite you in, take a quick peek at the Mac. If the Mac's outside case is open—they're tinkering. This is not a good sign.

If you were to find a soldering iron anywhere in the room, that's another troublesome sign. However, if you find a video card anywhere near the opened Mac, you must immediately dial 717 (this works on any telephone in the continental U.S.) and you'll be connected to the Macintosh user crisis line. Calmly give them your location, and the "PC user in disguise's" address. They'll dispatch a team of highly trained commandos who will rappel down the side of their house and into their home, extract the Mac unit, and replace it with a Compaq Presario. Don't feel bad—the person you're "turning in" will never really know the difference. They were on the wrong platform to begin with. They actually feel more comfortable surrounded by circuit board testers, tech support numbers, and virus eradication software. You're actually doing them a favor.

On the other hand, I truly believe there's a large segment of the PC population that *really* should be on the Mac platform. People who chose a PC because they really didn't have a choice. It's what their company uses, or what their best friend (neighbor, sister-in-law, etc.) uses, and they never really asked themselves the question "Am I a Mac person or a PC person?" They just knew they needed a computer, and everybody seems to have a PC, so that must be the thing to get, right?

That's why I put together the "Definitive Platform Test" to help you determine whether you or the people you know are on the right platform. If you're already a Macintosh user, go ahead and take the test—it will reaffirm the fact that you totally made the right choice. If you're a PC user taking the test, it might uncover that you're on the wrong platform for your particular personality, and you might be much happier on a Mac (or it might uncover the fact that you're so a PC person, that it freaks you out).

The Testing Environment

To take this test, you'll need to set up a proper testing environment. First, go into your desk drawer and get out a number 2 pencil. Ah-ha! See, that was a trick question—only PC users have things like number 2 pencils. That's because their therapists are constantly making them take written personality tests to prove their self-worth, which incidentally, they generally fail, or they'd be Mac users in the first place.

Next, lower the lights, put on some light jazz, and remove at least one article of clothing to set the mood. This is a multiple-choice test, and you're to choose the answer that most closely applies to you.

The Test

1. If you were in the video store to rent a video, which of these would you most likely rent?

❑ (a) *The Matrix*

❑ (b) *Godzilla* (the remake with Matthew Broderick)

❑ (c) *Battlefield Earth*

❑ (d) *Demented Death Farm Massacre*

2. Your dream mate would:

❑ (a) Be smart, funny, spontaneous, and understand the real you.

❑ (b) Be attractive, organized, focused on his/her career.

❑ (c) Be detail-oriented and wear sensible shoes.

❑ (d) Finally lift that restraining order.

3. You would describe your driving skills as:

❑ (a) Average, I'm not a bad driver.

❑ (b) I'm an excellent driver, very cautious and alert.

❑ (c) I obey all posted traffic signs and don't exceed the speed limit.

❑ (d) I wish all these idiots would just get off the road!

4. On a typical Saturday night, you're most likely to:

❑ (a) Go to a nightclub, party, or out with friends.

❑ (b) Clean the house, do laundry, and generally straighten up.

❑ (c) Optimize your hard drive, start doing your taxes early, and write a letter to the local newspaper complaining about the actions of the city council.

❏ (d) Sit in a car across the street from a co-worker's house with a telephoto lens, taking black-and-white photos, which you'll enlarge in your darkroom and tack to the kitchen wall in your dimly lit apartment.

5. A fun day for you might be:

❏ (a) Going to the beach.

❏ (b) Mowing the lawn, catching up on your bills, and cleaning out your garage.

❏ (c) Finding typos in a software manual, highlighting them with a yellow highlighter, and mailing it back to the company.

❏ (d) Watching from across the street as the police raid your apartment to confiscate your surveillance photos tacked to your kitchen wall of a co-worker.

6. You'd describe your friends as follows:

❏ (a) Fun, outgoing, and spontaneous people who love life.

❏ (b) Good solid people; predictable and down to earth.

❏ (c) They're serious, no-nonsense people. You always know where you stand with them; they don't play a lot of mind games.

❏ (d) He's a quiet man. Very polite, but a bit of a loner. Kind of keeps to himself.

7. How would you describe the company you work for?

❏ (a) It's a great, forward-thinking company that cares about my ideas and input, and it's a fun, creative work environment.

❑ (b) Not a bad company, and it's a steady paycheck, so I don't complain.

❑ (c) My boss is an idiot, and I know I could run the company better than she does.

❑ (d) I can tell they're plotting behind my back.

8. If you look in your closet, you're more likely to find:

❑ (a) T-shirts, jeans, sweaters, stuff from Old Navy

❑ (b) Polo shirts, Dockers, and stuff from The Gap

❑ (c) Business suits, dress shirts, nicely pressed pants, and stuff from Sears

❑ (d) Black ski masks, camouflage pants, combat boots, and stuff from Army/Navy surplus

9. On your desk at work, you're more likely to find:

❑ (a) An Oscar Mayer wiener whistle, a Palm organizer, and a Snickers bar

❑ (b) A *Stress Management for Dummies* book, a set of highlighters, and a high-protein nutrition snack

❑ (c) A Compaq hand-held organizer, a box of nicely sharpened pencils, a prescription for Tagamet

❑ (d) Grease paint, a machete, and a Slim Jim beef snack

10. Which of these bumper stickers would most likely wind up on your car?

❑ (a) Mean people suck.

❑ (b) Don't bother me, I'm having a bad day.

❑ (c) What are you looking at, stupid!

❑ (d) Honk if you're carrying an assault rifle.

11. Which of these TV reruns are you most likely to watch?

❑ (a) *Star Trek: The Next Generation*

❑ (b) *Family Matters*

❑ (c) CSPAN *Week in Review*

❑ (d) I don't watch TV.

12. Which of these jewelry items are you most likely to wear?

❑ (a) Toe ring

❑ (b) Expensive watch

❑ (c) Pocket watch

❑ (d) Dog tags

13. Which of these vehicles appeals to you most?

❑ (a) VW Beetle

❑ (b) Toyota Camry

❑ (c) Ford MiniVan

❑ (d) Humvee

14. Which of these are you most likely to do?

❑ (a) Obey Giant

❑ (b) Obey your parents

❑ (c) Obey posted speed limits

❑ (d) Obey the voices in your head

15. Which of these books are you most likely to read?

❑ (a) *Zen and the Art of Motorcycle Maintenance,* by Robert M. Pirsig

❑ (b) *So You Wish to Learn All About Economics,* by Lyndon LaRouche

❑ (c) *The Field Guide to Amphibians of Eastern and Central North America,* by Roger Conant, et al

❑ (d) *Stalkers and their Victims,* by Paul E Mullen

16. Which of these is your favorite ride at Disneyland/Disney World?

❑ (a) Space Mountain

❑ (b) The Train

❑ (c) It's a Small World

❑ (d) The parking lot tram

17. Which of these are you most likely to find in your purse/wallet?

❑ (a) Aerosmith concert ticket stubs

❑ (b) *Up With People* concert ticket stubs

❑ (c) Repair claim check from CompUSA

❑ (d) Pawn shop stub for a shoulder-mounted rocket launcher

18. Which of these are you most likely to find in your home?

❑ (a) A cappuccino maker

❑ (b) A Veg-a-matic

❑ (c) An automatic envelope sealer

❑ (d) A police scanner

19. If you had to choose one of the four jobs listed, which would you most likely choose?

❑ (a) President of a major TV network

❑ (b) Producer at the local PBS station

❑ (c) Actuary at an insurance company

❑ (d) Groundskeeper at the stadium

20. People who don't follow the crowd are:

❑ (a) Leaders, people who think differently.

❑ (b) Taking too big a risk.

❑ (c) Unstable and should be watched closely.

❑ (d) Making me very, very angry.

Scoring

The scoring for this test is as follows:

• For every question you answered (a), give yourself 5 points.

• For every question you answered (b), give yourself 3 points.

• For every question you answered (c), give yourself 2 points.

• For every question you answered (d), give yourself 1 point.

Tally your points and use the total for the following analysis.

Analysis

MAC PERSON: If you scored between 80 and 100, you are definitely a Mac person. You're a bright, creative, fun person, and you won't be happy with a computer that is anything less. You made the right choice to go Macintosh, and forcing you to use a PC would be cruel and unusual punishment.

It's a pretty good bet that you check the Mac news daily on the Web; you've got an Apple sticker on your car (or motorcycle); you like what Steve Jobs has done for Apple, but you don't like Steve as a person; you've been to (or are planning to visit) Apple's Company Store at their headquarters in Cupertino, California; and you have some Apple logo clothing (at least a black ball cap with the white Apple logo stitched on the front).

You probably know a little bit about Apple's history—maybe a lot—and you've been using a Mac for years and still haven't found a reason to buy a different video card. You use floppy disks as drink coasters, and you have a Think Different poster hanging in your bedroom. In short, you're cool, and people like you (at least, I would certainly like you).

BORDERLINE: If you scored between 60 and 80, you're on the Mac borderline. You're probably pretty happy with your Macintosh, but using a PC wouldn't freak you out.

You're not firmly committed to the Mac, and when it's time to buy a new computer you probably ask yourself the question, "Should I get another Mac, or should I look at the new PCs?" You're a nice person, a caring person, but you don't have much of a wild side. You pretty much like things to be orderly, you don't like a lot of surprises. You have to come to grips with the fact that you might be a closet PC user.

What you need is a tiebreaker. Go back and look at your answer to question 9. If you answered (a), you're still a solid Mac person, and have no need to worry. Rejoice in the splendor that is you. If you answered (b), you're still in that gray middle ground, and the tiebreaker didn't really help. Climb a nearby mountain and do some soul-searching. If you answered (c), I can't help you. If you answered (d), you need help, but I'm not qualified to help you.

PC USER: If you scored between 40 and 60, you're definitely a PC user, and if you're already using a PC, you're right where you need to be. You enjoy all the complexity and troubleshooting aspects of the Windows' world. It doesn't bother you being on virus watch 365 days a year, and you've got plenty of time at home to hang on the line for Microsoft tech support.

You're uptight, structured, and probably agitated a good amount of the time (and with good reason). You're the smart one, the one that "knows what's going on," and the people you work with, and your supervisors, they're just not nearly as smart as you are.

You prefer that a large multinational corporation tell you how things are supposed to be, what to buy, and you don't mind if that large multinational company keeps tabs on you and your computer. You're happy in the knowledge that you're not taking any chances— you're using "the industry standard" and nobody can fault you for that. You find troubleshooting a network a fun Saturday project.

You really don't understand "Mac people," and you think that computers that come in different colors are silly. You're not likely to vacation in France or own a convertible. You probably drive a brown car, live in a beige house, and have 2.5 kids. You find Thai food offensive and can't understand the music that kids these days are listening to. It's not real music, like the kind you listened to when you were a kid.

MISUNDERSTOOD LONER: If you scored between 20 and 40, you're a militant PC user. You may as well go ahead and remove Windows from your PC altogether, and install a fresh copy of DOS (after all, those silly icons and the Start menu are really beginning to upset you—especially at night when they come to life and tell you to do bad things).

While you're at it, probably the best advice I can give you at this point is to put your hands on your head, walk out the front door of your home directly toward the officers, and listen carefully to their instructions. Keep your hands clearly in sight and don't make any sudden moves.

Summary

My guess is, if you bought this book, you easily scored between 80 and 100.

There is another layer of Macintosh user that is also perfectly acceptable—the layer that uses a Macintosh, but doesn't really get into the Mac experience. For example, the Subway sandwich shops in my area use Macs for their cash registers. Each day, every sandwich artist at these Subway stores uses a Mac, but they're not all "into" the Mac, so you can't really call them "Mac people." But in my mind, anyone who makes yummy sandwiches can't be all bad, so I pretty much let them off the hook. Hopefully their exposure to the Mac will make them less reluctant to try a Mac when they buy their next computer.

Now, I do need to address one last issue regarding this platform test: What should you do if you answered (d) three or more times, but still scored above 40? The only way to really find out if you're carrying some serious baggage is to wait until dark, wear lots of camouflage, and climb into a tower....

How to resist the overwhelming temptation to strangle Apple's management

There is a moment that occurs in most every Mac user's life that will change you forever. Years later, you'll probably remember where you were when it happened, and what you saw, heard, or read that *made* it happen; but when it happens—you'll know it. It's that magic moment when you make the jump from casual Mac user to real Mac fanatic. It happens almost in an instant, but once you step through that door, there's no coming back. That magic moment occurs the first time you seriously criticize Apple's management. Now you're one of us. Now you care.

Before that moment, what Apple did, how Apple stock is doing, which new machines they introduce, and their latest ad campaign is all pretty much meaningless to you. Up until that moment, you see

Apple pretty much the way the rest of the PC world sees Apple—as another computer company. But suddenly, in one instant, they're not just a computer company to you anymore. Now, what happens to Apple matters. You care.

At that moment, on either a conscious or subconscious level, you realize that if Apple were to go out of business, your life would be affected. If they screw up—you're screwed. Because now your Macintosh is more to you than just a computer. You may have used a computer for years, and you always just "used a computer," but this is different. It's the kind of "different" that's hard, if not impossible, to describe to non-Mac users. But you know that it's different with every fiber in your Mueslix; this is definitely a different experience.

But you also know, on some level, that at least one part of your newfound happiness is in danger. It's in danger of Apple's doing something so stupid that they go out of business (which obviously has never happened, but it still freaks you out). You see, if Apple were to go out of business, it would definitely impact your life, because you love your Macintosh. Having to use a PC is no longer an option. You're past that. On to something new, something better. You're now standing on third base; you don't want to go back to second.

You've realized that using a PC is, well, just using a computer. But using a Macintosh is fun. You don't want the fun to end, and that's why now, when you read a news report, or see a lightweight Apple ad on TV, you think, "Oh my God, they're totally screwing up! My grandmother could come up with a better ad than that! We've got to do something!" and there it was—that moment where you crossed over from being a generally disinterested Mac owner, to an intensely caring Mac fanatic, who's now totally annoyed with Apple's management. Welcome aboard. We've been expecting you.

Now, I have to warn you, watching Apple management make decisions can be a lot like watching your favorite football team when they're behind by 17 points late in the fourth quarter, and they're running tight ends up the middle when they're on their own 20. You'll be doing a lot of yelling. Second-guessing Apple's every move is like being an armchair quarterback, but the difference is, you'd actually be much better running Apple than you probably would be as a quarterback in the NFL, and that makes it even more frustrating.

You're going to use words to describe their mistakes that you haven't used since you accidentally closed the car door on your fingers (you've done that, right?). You'll find that second-guessing Apple is the number-one favorite pastime at Macintosh User Groups, Internet Cafes, or wherever real Mac fanatics congregate. This is the bond that keeps us together—a devotion to a company that makes such colossal mistakes, it makes you want to scream until you're just an empty head of sockets.

Apple, as a corporation, is a lot like your own children. As your children grow up, you see them about to make mistakes, perhaps mistakes you made as a child or teenager. These "potholes in the road of life" seem so clear to you now; and when you see your kids heading in that direction, you feel it's your duty as a parent to try to stop them, and give them the benefit of your experience. But alas, your kids (my kids, everyone's kids) just won't listen. Why? Because they think they know better (just like Apple's management). So all you can do is sit back and watch them make the mistakes. Watching this happen is incredibly frustrating, because you know you could've helped them if (insert angelic bell sound effect here) "only they'd listen."

This is exactly how you'll feel about Apple. Trust me. You'll see them introduce a product, or start another artsy ad campaign, or do one of the million things they do without thinking 30 seconds into the future, and you'll want to pick up the phone and call Apple's management and say, "Wait! Stop! You're about to make a huge mistake!" But Apple won't take your call. Why? Because Apple knows better. This is why, according to a study released by the American Board of Unnecessary Stress, Apple has now officially replaced teenagers as the leading cause of premature gray hair in adults aged 35 to 40.

You see, here's the problem. Take a company that makes refrigerators—we'll use Amana for example. I'm sure Amana is a fine company, and I'm sure they make a fine product. But I have to be honest with you—if Amana went out of business, I'd certainly feel bad for the people who work at Amana, but outside of that I really wouldn't care. When it came time to get a new refrigerator, I'd get a Kenmore, a Maytag, or a Whirlpool. Now, my refrigerator keeps my food cold and fresh, and I need food to survive (apparently, quite a lot of it) and so because my refrigerator is actually tied to my survival on some level, you'd figure I'd be an Amana fanatic. I'd be tracking Amana stock daily, checking out any breaking news on the Web about Amana, and if Amana should introduce a model of refrigerator I don't particularly like, or feel they shouldn't have introduced, then I'd be heading straight for an online newsgroup to join with other Amana refrigerator fanatics where we'd all collectively give Amana a good tongue-lashing for doing something so dumb. It sounds crazy doesn't it? It does when it's a refrigerator (even though my refrigerator is often the source of much happiness in my home, especially the freezer section where I keep the ice cream).

So why is fanaticism about Apple okay, but silly when it's about Amana? It's because (and again, nothing against Amana), Amana makes a refrigerator that is more or less pretty much like all other refrigerators. An example would be that Dell makes a PC that's pretty much like a Gateway or an HP. They essentially do the same thing, in essentially the same way.

Whether you buy a Gateway, HP, or Dell (customer service issues aside), your computing experience is going to be almost exactly identical. In fact, if you hid the computers behind a desk and attached three identical monitors, one to each machine, it would be virtually impossible for the average person to look at the monitor and tell you whether the image they saw on that monitor was being powered by a Dell, a Gateway, or an HP. Same thing with a milk carton from any refrigerator—if I poured three glasses of milk, and each glass had the same brand of milk (think Windows here), there would be no way for the person drinking one to say, "Oh, this milk definitely came from the Kenmore" (although someone at Kenmore may take issue with that). All three are the same experience—cold milk from a good refrigerator.

Well, that's what's different about Macintosh. It's not the same experience. It's different. Vastly different. Although at first glance someone who has never used a Mac might think Macintosh and Windows are very much the same (they both use icons, control panels, a trash can/recycle bin, etc.), ask anyone who has switched over to Macintosh about what a HUGE difference there really is.

After all, since there's easily 10 times more software for the PC, and a much larger hardware selection, and PCs are cheaper to buy, and they're available virtually everywhere, why in the world would someone leave all that? There must be a reason! There is, and that's why every year, thousands of PC users "jump ship" and come over to the Mac. It's not just because it's easier—they already know how to use a computer—they're already PC users, so there's got to be something more. There is, but explaining the difference to a PC user is like trying to describe the color blue to a blind man. You really just have to use one to know, and shortly after you do, and if you use one long enough, I guarantee you'll start to criticize Apple's management, you'll get numerous ulcers, and eventually your hair will start to turn gray. The amazing thing is—it's all worth it (okay, not the gray hair part).

Thus far we've looked a little bit at what's going to happen to you, and why it's going to happen to you. But now I have the task of telling you *how* it's going to happen to you (at least, from a historical perspective; but at Apple, history continually repeats itself), *and* how to handle it in a way that keeps you from gobbling Zantac like peanut M&Ms.

What's going to happen:

You're watching TV one night. A commercial comes on, and you don't really pay much attention to it, because it's stupid, makes no sense, and you can't even figure out what the ad, is trying to sell. You figure it's either (a) a cellular phone ad, (b) the last of the "dot com" ads, or (c) a perfume/cologne ad. But then at the very end, you see the Apple logo and the words "Think different." You say the same thing that the Super Bowl TV announcers said immediately after the ad aired introducing the original Macintosh back in 1984: "What the hell was that?" You'll follow it up with "That was an Apple ad? I don't get it. Nobody's gonna get it. How in the world would a Windows user see that ad and want to switch to Macintosh? That absolutely sucks!" You'll go on and on until your phone rings. It's one of your Mac buddies: "Did you see the Apple ad? What a piece of crap!" That same scenario is playing over and over again, all across the country, as outraged Mac fanatics call one another to express, well…their outrage. This is the way it's always been.

Actually at this point in time we're lucky. The agency that Apple has been using for the past few years is TBWA/Chiat Day, and I have to say, in my opinion they blow away Apple's previous agency, BBDO. In fact, I don't think you can compare the two. Overall, I think TBWA has done a pretty darn good job.

So now that Apple has changed agencies, but there are still some very funky ads, you realize the problem must not be at the agency—it's with Apple management. After all, Apple has to approve the ads. TBWA/Chiat Day doesn't just secretly produce and run ads and then send Apple a bill, so I place the blame for ads that make you go "Hmmmmm?" squarely on Apple. Especially back in the old days with BBDO.

I remember an ad that got me so mad it made me seriously question my allegiance to Apple. In a hopping mad editorial I subsequently wrote in *Mac Today,* I called the ad "The $1,400 alarm clock." After seeing it air on TV, I wrote in the magazine, "…four well-respected top Apple executives are now gone, but amazingly the executive in charge of Apple's domestic advertising is somehow still there. It's more than amazing—it has to be a merciful act of God, because I can't imagine that anyone with a brain larger than a hamster's would buy a Mac after seeing that ad."

The 30-second spot featured a shot of a 12-year-old boy asleep in his bedroom one morning. Suddenly, his Mac "goes off" like an alarm clock and plays an MTV-style QuickTime movie yelling at him to "Wake Up!" The kid finally wakes up, stumbles over to his Mac, hits a key (presumably a computer snooze button), and the annoying QuickTime movie stops. Then he falls back into bed to catch a few more Zzzzzz's. Apple logo. The end.

What could Apple have been thinking? Did they really believe that parents would think, "Hey, that's great! I'll spend $1,400 (that's what they cost back then) so my kid can wake up to a QuickTime movie!"?

At the same time, Microsoft was running a series of ads showing two teenage girls using Microsoft Encarta on their PC to help them study. It showed movies (of bacteria splitting) on their computer, with the background info of Botticelli's *The Birth of Venus,* and the kids laughing and quizzing each other back and forth. Now, I could see how parents watching that Microsoft ad might think, "Hey, I wonder if buying a PC would make studying more fun for my daughter." But I just can't see how that Apple ad would sell even one unit, where a parent had a role in the buying decision (and at $1,400, I imagine most 12-year-olds are going to have to lean on their parents for computing cash).

What else can you expect in Apple-approved ads? Traditionally, in Apple ads you can expect to see an awful lot of the outside of a Mac. Shots from the front. Shots from the side. The Mac rotating on an unseen pedestal, but you'll see little of the Mac's screen, and its amazing software in action. For some reason, Apple has this thing about showing the outside of the Macintosh (which looks nice), rather than the Mac software (which is what really separates it from a PC).

Don't get me wrong, Macs are hands-down the best-looking computers on the planet, and I love the way they look. But unfortunately, that's not where the magic of the Macintosh lies. The thing that makes people fall in love with their Macs is the operating system. That and the fact that to this day, it's still the only real plug-and-play platform. Here's what I've always felt: Our machine looks better than their machine, but that's just not enough to get most people to switch platforms. But show them things that the Macintosh can do that their computer can't do, and now you've given them something to think about.

Show them parts of the OS that are better, that are more powerful, that are more fun, and that make using the Macintosh something really special. Show how to install a font, connect a printer, or do one of the myriad of things that a Mac does faster, easier, and better than Windows does to this very day. Make people watching at home think "Hey, that Macintosh looks pretty cool." If Apple could do that, then we'd stop yelling at the screen (and PC users might give Macs a second look).

Apple did give viewers a quick glimpse of the power of Macintosh software with their iMovie ads for the iMac. Mind you, they could've blown people away with the ads, but they decided to show the software for a few seconds, and then the outside of the computer for the rest of the time. It drives me nuts. A Macintosh is not just the outside of the box; it's the combination of the software and hardware that makes a Mac. The box itself is just a good-looking plastic enclosure that holds the best operating system ever.

Here's the problem in a nutshell: Mac fanatics want hard-hitting ads. They want ads that show the power and wonder of the Mac, and they feel if Apple can come up with those, it will make all the difference. I've been watching Apple ads for more than a decade, and as best as I can tell, Apple hasn't had a lot of those (and they've had every opportunity to achieve ad greatness).

For example, when Apple introduced the G4, it was so fast that the U.S. government classified it as a supercomputer, which meant that the Pentagon would automatically put restrictions on which foreign governments could buy one. That's the kind of marketing bonanza most companies dream of.

So Apple created a TV spot that could have been an absolute home run, if they had changed just one thing (as you'll see in a moment). The spot starts with military music in the background and a close-up of the G4 tower. A military-sounding narrator says, "For the first time in history, a computer has been classified as a weapon by the U.S. Government." As he says this, a tank's treads pass behind the G4. The narrator continues, "With the power to perform over 1 billion calculations per second, the Pentagon doesn't want it to fall into the wrong hands." As this is happening, U.S. Army tanks move into position around the G4. The voiceover continues, "As for Pentium PCs, well…they're harmless." As the camera pulls back, the G4 is surrounded by five tanks, with their gun turrets pointing outward as if they're protecting the G4. The spot ends with the standard closing: Apple logo and "Think different." Sounds pretty cute doesn't it? I have to admit, it was very well produced too. The only problem? PC users didn't get it. Everyone I talked to about the ad thought that the whole concept wasn't serious, because the ad called it a *weapon*. I explained that it was the truth, and the reason that it was considered a "weapon" was because of its speed; it was the first personal computer officially classified as a "supercomputer," and therefore it couldn't be sold to unfriendly foreign governments. Then they immediately "got it" and said (I'm paraphrasing here) "Wow, is it really? It's that fast?" Every PC person I talked with about it had seen the ad (Apple ran it on virtually every prime time show for weeks), but not one of them "got it," until that moment. Just one word changed, and it goes from big miss to huge hit! That was one expensive word.

So, does Apple ever have a good TV ad? They've had a couple. I thought their ad touting the fact that the Mac was immune to the Y2K bug was outstanding. It featured HAL, the computer from *2001: A Space Odyssey*. It was very clever, kept you watching, and most importantly it really made its point. So what's not to like? Apple ran it only once—during the 1999 Super Bowl. If you missed it, well…you missed it. This ad should've been running in prime time for weeks, but no such luck. They took one shot, and if the message didn't get out, well, too bad (too bad for us, anyway).

The one ad I would have to say was a home run (besides the award-winning "1984" ad that introduced the original Macintosh, of course) was the ad with a snail carrying a Pentium chip on its back, set to old-time music. You didn't need to say a word—the clever visual said it all, and helped (for the first time ever) to really start to put to rest the misconception that Macs are slower than PCs.

Why it happens:

Apparently, only companies like Dell and Gateway are allowed to run hard-hitting computer ads.

What's going to happen:

Apple makes a marketing decision that defies simple logic.

For example, how about naming OS 10 "OS X"? It was a cool name. Until Apple had to release a maintenance upgrade shortly after OS X's release. Now, what were they going to name it? "Mac OS X.1?" Of course not, because X is a Roman numeral, but 1 isn't. So, Mac OS X become OS 10.1 in no time.

Seriously, who thought naming it OS X was going to be a good idea? When it was introduced, most people I know called the original release OS X (the letter "X") because that's exactly what it looks like. Besides, Apple had never used a Roman numeral before to name an OS, so why would they change it now? Also, every time it appears in print, it appears as an "X," unless Apple could somehow convince the media to include the tag line "Oh, by the way, that's the Roman numeral Ten."

Once the maintenance release came, any branding Apple might have built with the OS X name was gone, because then there was a new operating system called 10.1. This is the stuff that keeps me up at night.

This isn't the first time Apple made me scratch my head over a marketing decision (and I'm sure not the last). Perhaps an even bigger marketing bungle, only because it continued for so long, is the fact that the Apple logo appeared upside down on every open PowerBook and iBook for years.

Now think about it—why is there a big ol' Apple logo on the back of every PowerBook? Why else? It's advertising for Apple, and why not? Having a big Apple logo on the back of the PowerBook makes perfect marketing sense. It's having it appear upside down when in use that is totally and utterly senseless.

Imagine how frustrating this must be for the department at Apple that handles product placement (getting Apple computers on TV and in movies). They got placement deals in huge theatrical hits, such as *Independence Day, Mission Impossible,* and *Jurassic Park,* and every time you saw a PowerBook in use on the big screen, you saw the Apple logo upside down.

Now, could you imagine a company like GM, Disney, or Pepsi putting their logo on a product so that when its in use, it appears upside down? Worse, could you imagine these companies paying to have their upside-down logo appear in a movie? Of course not, but somehow Apple let this go on for years. Now, want to really get your mug frosted? Check this out: When introducing a new updated model of the G3 PowerBook, Apple decided to do a very cool thing—they backlit the Apple logo. *Very* cool! But can you believe it, they left the logo upside-freakin' down! I just couldn't believe it.

Apple finally flipped the logos right-side-up when they introduced the second round of iBooks, and on the G4 Titanium PowerBooks— which could be nothing more than an admission that leaving them upside down for years was whacked.

What's going to happen:

Apple's going to introduce a product that makes no sense to you, like the Cube, and you're going to go off like a Roman candle.

What to do about it:

Nothing. Don't get upset. Just "let it go" and continue living life as you always have. When Apple introduced the Cube, many Mac people lost their minds. These users attacked it head on—in the press, on the Web, on upturned boxes in the town square, with a vengeance I've not seen before or since. What happened was simple—Apple introduced a new machine for a specific market: trendy, looks-conscious executives, and upscale home users, both of whom would appreciate its very small size, near-silent operation, and lack of the clutter normally associated with having a computer on your desk. This new Cube was an engineering marvel. It won award after award, but that couldn't save it from the wrath of angry Mac users who acted as if Apple had announced, "This new Cube will replace ALL Macintosh models from this point forward" (which they certainly didn't). I think the main reason they did it wasn't because the Cube was so bad, I think it was because it just wasn't what *they* wanted. *They* wanted a 17" iMac, but what they got was the Cube, so they beat it into the ground, and before long Apple had a warehouse full, with no buyers. This is called "Shooting ourselves in the foot."

I think of it this way: If I own a Ford Taurus and Ford introduces a Taurus Wagon, what do I care? Even if I'll never buy one, it's just another model in the line—it doesn't affect me. But what happened to the Cube is that it fell victim to our overzealousness to nail Apple on a product we (Mac fanatics) saw as a mistake. In effect, we "killed the Cube" even before Apple had a chance to. I can't blame the fans because they felt very strongly about the Cube—they feel strongly about everything Apple-related, and it's those people (you, me, we, they) that have kept Apple in business in spite of Apple management.

Now that cooler heads prevail, my previous advice stands—if Apple introduces a product that makes no sense to you whatsoever and you feel it's a huge mistake, just "let it go."

What's going to happen:

Apple will show off a new look for its operating system so far in advance of its shipping that when it does finally ship, it looks dated. Worse than that, since they "tip their hand" on the new look, some slick software designers will almost immediately come up with appearance schemes that will make your Mac look exactly like the "unreleased" operating system today, even though the real thing may not be shipping for a year or more (if ever).

It's happened more than once. Years ago Apple was working on a new operating system code-named Copland. They gave the press a preview of its cool new look and before you knew it, it was on the cover of every Mac magazine on the planet. Within a few days of those magazines hitting the newsstands you could go on AOL and download similar-looking icons and fonts, and within a couple of weeks there was a shareware control panel you could download to give your old Mac the new look, just by installing the control panel and rebooting.

As it turned out, most of the cool look of Copland never material-ized when they shipped Mac OS 8 (which is what happened in place of Copland), and even if it had, everyone's machines had the Copland look for a year before that. The look was "played."

You'd think Apple would have learned from this mistake, but it happened again, years later, when they showed off the interface for Mac OS X. People were able to come up with Appearance Schemes that were even easier to implement than the Copland Schemes, because of Apple's Appearance Control Panel, and within about 30 seconds, your Mac, running OS 8.6, 9.0, or 9.1, suddenly looked like Mac OS X, right down to the folder icons, status bars, buttons, and all. So, when you finally upgrade to Mac OS X, the look is nothing to get excited about—it's old hat.

What to do about it:

Don't use these Appearance Control Panels that mimic the upcoming system because it will take away a big part of the fun that a major upgrade offers—the look and feel.

What's going to happen:

When Apple doesn't really have a new look for one of their existing designs and it's time for Steve Jobs to make a big splash at the Macworld Expo keynote, Apple will change the color slightly on an existing computer, when you were hoping and praying for a cool new design.

What to do about it:

Get used to it. In the absence of real innovation, brightly colored plastic will apparently step right in.

What's going to happen:

Apple is going to introduce so many different models that it
will become nearly impossible for you to tell a friend which model
to buy.

Here's how history has begun to repeat itself: When Steve Jobs
came back to Apple, one of his big gripes was that there were so
many different Mac models, it made it incredibly confusing to the
buying public (not to mention salespeople, the press, even Apple
employees). So Steve slashed the product line almost immediately,
but his real stroke of genius was to replace the entire low-end
product line with just one unit—the iMac.

It was brilliant. If you wanted an iMac, you just went to the store
and said, "I want an iMac." You didn't have to worry about which
iMac you wanted because there was only one model. It worked
astoundingly well—finally, consumers knew exactly which Apple
model they wanted. When Steve introduced the five different iMac
colors, it didn't create confusion—it created choice (and a headache
for all of Apple's competitors). The beauty of his plan—it was still
just one model, but now you had your choice of colors, and people
absolutely loved that. In fact, it changed the whole PC industry,
which rushed to try to emulate Apple's transparent plastic colors.

Ah, but you knew that kind of success couldn't last forever. Soon,
Apple started introducing "Special Edition" iMacs, and DV iMacs,
and iMacs with a different set of colors, and a different set of specs,
and before long the model confusion that the iMac was supposed to
eliminate was brought back with a vengeance. To this day, I'd have to
do some serious research about which iMac model to suggest for a

friend, because I'm not sure which configurations are available, and once we do figure out which configuration is right for them, then we have to see if Apple offers it in the color they want, because not all colors are available for every configuration. The result: Product confusion is once again the order of the day.

What to do about it:

If you want an iMac, be flexible and don't get mentally married to one color scheme, because when you find the configuration you want, it's probably not available in that color.

What's going to happen:

Apple will suddenly change their mind about just about anything.

For example:

Apple has a history of creating a product, getting lots of people to adopt it, and then suddenly, without warning—it's gone. For example, remember those really cool-looking Apple Studio Displays that I mentioned earlier that had a clear case? The one Apple introduced at the same time as the Cube? I personally thought that they were the best-looking monitors Apple had ever made. Which was why I was so surprised that Apple discontinued them (Apple now sells only flat-panel monitors).

This discontinued beauty wasn't a big seller because of (don't get me started again) its nonstandard connectors. But my point is—one day it's there—for sale at the Apple Online Store—the next day it's gone forever.

Another instance of Apple changing its mind happened back when Steve Jobs first returned to Apple, and he decided to pull the plug on "Mac clones." That's right, you used to be able to buy a Macintosh from companies other than Apple (Gasp!). You could buy them from Motorola, UMAX, Power Computing, and a couple of others, but Steve thought that the Mac OS licensing deal put together by his predecessors amounted to a bad deal for Apple, so he "killed the clones." Mac users pitched a royal fit, but really, what could they do? Steve's a moving target. (And a billionaire, which probably means, like all billionaires, he has a mob of evil henchmen who wear black berets and striped soccer shirts, and they hang out in his secret hidden lair asking questions like "Whatda we do now, boss?")

Another popular Apple product was quietly laid to rest when Apple stopped producing printers. Apple was in the printer business big-time for years, with Apple LaserWriters (remember them?) and StyleWriter inkjet printers, then just a few years ago they quietly slipped into the night. Here one day, gone the next.

Another case of Apple changing their mind was introducing dual-processor Macs at Macworld Expo and then, shortly thereafter, discontinuing them; and then at the following Macworld Expo, reintroducing them yet again. Was it a chip shortage or a brain shortage?

You can go back and dig up other instances of Apple introducing a product and then smothering it with a pillow when nobody's looking. Remember the cool-looking QuickTake digital camera? Went away without much fanfare. Also, the Newton, Apple's shot at a handheld PDA that could be held only by people with very large hands, and a shirt pocket the size of a pillow case. But honestly, the Newton going away was more of a mercy killing.

To give you an insight into why the Newton failed, look to Apple management. Their research showed that the reason some people didn't use computers is that they were intimidated by them. As they dug a bit deeper, their research showed that what intimidated them most was the keyboard, so Apple came up with the first real PDA, which used a pen instead of a keyboard. The idea was that it would recognize your handwriting. That was the idea, but in reality I never found a person's handwriting that it really recognized. You would write "Meeting with Dan at 8:00 a.m. on Wednesday," and the Newton would interpret your handwriting as "Neblock chee ponri 60 ham."

In addition to the fact that it possessed the handwriting recognition capabilities of a squirrel, it was so large that Apple recommended seeing a chiropractor within 24 hours of carrying it to your car. But the biggest problem wasn't its shortcomings—it was the people who bought it. Instead of all these "I'm-intimidated-by-computers" people buying Newtons, you know who bought Newtons? Mac users (of course). That's right, the people who bought the Newton were primarily people who already owned computers—Apple computers.

The Newton never caught on with the intimidated general public it was originally designed to attract. As subsequent versions of the Newton were released, the Newton got somewhat better. (I know what you're thinking "They introduced subsequent versions?") Absolutely. They had to. They invested more on the development of

Newton than the gross national product of Finland, and they had to earn it back, even if it meant spending even more and more money and Apple's CFO passed out cold.

What did Apple management learn from this experience? Apple's product research needs some serious work, because what their research failed to uncover was this: People didn't really want a computer they could hold in their hand (which is essentially what the Newton was); they wanted an address book/to-do list/calendar they could easily fit in their purse or shirt pocket. Palm figured this out, and the rest is, as they say, history.

One product that really was a beauty, and is still popular with some longtime Mac fans, was the PowerBook 2400c. What makes this long-discontinued PowerBook remain in demand by some today? It was a sub-notebook. Although Apple never called it a sub-notebook, it was a small, super-thin unit that makes today's iBooks and Titaniums look huge in comparison. I had forgotten how small they were, but I was in L.A. teaching a seminar, and one of the attendees sitting in the front row was taking notes on a 2400c, and between classes I went over and checked it out. I was amazed all over again. It's so small, so thin, that I can't believe Apple hasn't been able to come up with a sub-notebook since.

What to do about it:

Know that whatever product you buy, Apple is likely to change their mind about it at some point, no matter how committed they may seem to be at its introduction.

What's going to happen:

Apple will try to introduce another consumer product.

For example:

Every so often, Apple decides to try to introduce a consumer product. Do you remember hearing about the Apple Pippin game machine? It was another of Apple's ill-fated attempts to go outside what they do best: to create a product that yet again, only Mac users will buy. The general public doesn't buy stuff from Apple. Mac users, the Mac faithful, and fans of Apple buy products with the Apple logo on them, and that's pretty much it.

It was back in 1996 when Apple tried to launch this product, which would connect to a TV set and let you play games and surf the Web with (get this) a 14.4 modem. Development started in 1993, and Apple spent a boatload of time and money on this new game box named Pippin (a name that, if uttered on the local playground, would surely get your butt whipped), and although it never made it in any numbers as far as the U.S., I understand that Apple did ship more than 20 units in Japan, where it was first introduced. Let's see…an Apple game machine, coupled with a 14.4 modem, going up against Nintendo, Sega, and Sony PlayStation? Good plan!

Apple also came up with a cool-looking, all-black, portable CD Player called the "Apple PowerCD" (long since gone), and an online service to compete with AOL called "eWorld" which evaporated after about a year due to severe lack of interest (although it was beautifully designed).

For some reason, even with its track record on marketing a consumer product, Apple just can't stay out of the consumer pool, and they introduced the iPod (Portable open database). It's a slick-looking, small, MP3 music player with a FireWire connector, that lets you download MP3s from your Mac into your iPod in seconds and take your tunes on the road. Of Apple's consumer products, I would say this is clearly their best effort yet, but when Apple introduced it, they ensured that *only Mac users* would buy it (like all Apple "consumer products" before it) by releasing only a Mac-compatible version—although they announced that a PC-compatible version was "in the works." In the meantime, other companies started introducing software so you could use a PC with the iPod. Therefore, when Apple finally introduces their PC version, it may already be "old news." How will the iPod fare? Well, every person that I know personally who has bought one, to this day is (you guessed it) a Macintosh user.

What to do about it:

Don't get sucked into the initial rush to buy the cool new Apple product. Sit back, relax, and see how it shakes out after a few months. If you're afraid the product might get discontinued, and that you'll be "stuck holding the bag," I hate to say it, but history is on your side.

What's going to happen:

Apple will try to sell Macs using a new method that seems like a good idea at the time; but then it will hit the ground with an enormous thud.

For example:

For years and years, when people bought Macs they bought them
from Apple dealers of one sort or another (a local reseller, authorized
mail order dealer, etc.). Then Apple decided to open the floodgates
and let virtually anybody sell Macs: Circuit City, Best Buy, Sears,
Montgomery Ward (before they went under), Office Depot, Staples,
and I even saw them for sale at Sam's Club (owned by Wal-Mart).

It was great that Macs were available all over town for a while, but
the common complaint from Mac users was that the Mac sections of
these stores were often (okay, usually) in total disarray. Macs were
turned off, broken, or otherwise inoperable, and the Mac sections
often looked so abandoned that most of us thought those sections
were probably doing Apple more harm than good.

It was a fairly common practice for some Mac fanatics from the
local user group to get together on a Saturday and go to every Sears,
Circuit City, Office Depot, etc., and quietly fix up the Mac section.
They would restart all the computers, start the self-running demos
on all the machines, and generally clean the place up and make it
look respectable. They usually had to do this on the sly because
as a general rule, the Mac department was staffed by—that's right—
PC users.

If you walked in and pointed to the Mac you wanted, knew exactly
the peripherals and extras you wanted, and didn't have any questions
for the salesperson, you stood a reasonable chance of getting out of
the store with a Mac. However, if you asked any questions, or showed
the slightest bit of hesitancy, the PC salesman would say something
like, "Are you sure you want a Mac?" or one of a dozen statements
that would make the potential Mac person feel that they were

making a mistake. Since the PC salesperson knows PCs inside and out, he/she would gladly steer you over to the PC section, and out you go with a Compaq Presario, when you came in asking about Macs.

Luckily, Steve Jobs learned of this Mac retail graveyard, yanked Macs out of just about every big chain, and started the very successful "Apple Store within a Store" concept with nationwide computer retailer CompUSA.

After the success of that, Apple is now quietly showing up back in other stores, like Circuit City, so expect the cycle to continue. Incidentally, I was in Circuit City last week, strolled over to the iMac section, and a PC salesman came over and asked if he could help. I just left (at least the self-running iMac demo was up and running).

Apple came up with another scheme for selling Macs, which would help with the fact that there were (at that time, around 1995) so many Mac models, even Apple employees couldn't keep up with which were which.

The idea was to create a line of Macs specifically for home users called the Performa line. This was an Apple marketing masterpiece (read nightmare).

Apple created this entire line for home users, and included free software for home users. The problem was that they would sell a model with virtually the same hardware features and overall look to business users, under the name Power Mac. What ensued was marketing chaos, with consumers constantly asking, "Well, what's the difference between the Performa 6110CD and the Power Mac 6100?" Under the hood, there was little difference, if any, but the perception was that Performas were less powerful, basically for kids and parents;

and the real power was (of course) in the Power Mac line (even though inside they were identical machines). In fact, sometimes the Performa machine was a better price than its Power Mac counterpart with the same specs, but again the perception was that Performas were less powerful, and, in my opinion, it pretty much doomed the line. Not to mention the fact that although the Performa line was designed to help consumers choose the right Mac, Apple almost defied them to try, by introducing more than 70 Performa models.

As badly implemented as the Performa concept was, the height of my embarrassment as a Mac user came during this era in late 1996, when Apple decided to produce a late-night TV infomercial to sell Performas.

The plot centered around a family considering buying a computer, but the burning question is "Will they use it?" Dad buys a Macintosh Performa, and gives them a week to see if they will indeed use it. Of course, they all use it daily, and it changes their lives forever. Yes, in just one week these seemingly ordinary people's lives were transformed: Dad makes money in the stock market, Mom designs greeting cards on her Mac and markets them to a huge greeting card company, and the son's math grades go up. But it's Grandpa who really comes out the winner (as you'll learn in a moment).

Grandpa's fortunes change as a knock is heard at the door and the "apparently-desperate-for-human-contact" family all race to the front door simultaneously. They open it, and there stands an attractive, well-dressed older woman. Grandpa asks, "Are you Rose?" She smiles and replies, "Yes," and Grandpa says, "Come in, come in." The family seems a bit stunned that Grandpa, who probably hasn't been out of the house since the late 1950s, suddenly has a female visitor.

Finally, Mom breaks the awkward silence and asks, "Grandpa, how did you two meet?" He replies, "We met online in the opera lover's forum" (Dear Lord, Grandpa is cruising for chicks in chat rooms). It gets worse.

Just after the family met Rose and she stepped into the house, there was a moment where I started laughing so hard my wife almost had to initiate CPR. Now get this: Once inside, Rose looked at Grandpa, and the first words out of her mouth were, "How much RAM do you have?" I almost died. I'm certain I at least blacked out more than once. I had almost caught my breath when Grandpa answered, "Eight meg," and Rose turned on a big smile and said, "I knew you were a power user." (I swear, I'm not making this stuff up.) I was rolling on the floor, laughing uncontrollably, fading in and out of consciousness for about 20 minutes. I couldn't do anything with a straight face for an entire week.

The infomercial, from top to bottom, was abysmal by anyone's standards, worse than an episode of "The Facts of Life." The acting was painfully bad, the dialog could only have been written by the collective talents of a third-grade class, and the premise of the infomercial was as well thought out as the idea to offer Performa models in the first place.

I can only imagine that after this infomercial aired, Apple management had to add extra security personnel and bodyguards to keep longtime loyalists from stringing them up by their heels. I never saw another Apple infomercial, and that's sad, because even though I'm confident it didn't sell one single unit, I have to say, I had one hell of a good laugh.

What's going to happen:

Apple does something that makes you wonder, "Didn't anybody think about this, or test this, or give this at least 30 seconds of thought?"

For example:

When Apple shipped the original iMac, the mouse that they shipped with it could only be described as "designed by Microsoft." It looked good—it just didn't work worth a darn. Take away its good looks, and it's what you would imagine a Soviet-era mouse would be like—clunky and awkward. It was shaped like a hockey puck (which should have tipped somebody off), and because it was perfectly round, you never knew which way was up when you grabbed it. Each time you did, your pointer would move in some weird direction for a moment or two, until you could straighten it out. It really made you wonder, "Did anybody ever test this thing?"

How popular was this hockey-puck mouse? Third-party vendors almost immediately began creating slip-on covers you could put over your heinous hockey puck to make it work like a regular mouse. This mouse was an affront to humanity, and most companies would have immediately replaced it with something better. After a million or so iMacs had been sold, and people all over the world were cussing their hockey pucks, Apple did introduce a new optical mouse, which I must admit looks and works beautifully. However, I still see these hockey pucks almost daily, usually with a plastic add-on cover to help hide Apple's shame.

Another thing that makes you wonder is why, after all the years of having the advantage of starting your computer from your keyboard (which is a Mac-only advantage by the way), Apple starts shipping keyboards with no "on" button. Well thought out.

Another classic example was the batteries on the old PowerBook 5300 series. After a while, some caught fire. That's usually not considered something that users enjoy. A little extra testing might have uncovered that "special hidden feature" but hey, what's a little fire between friends, eh?

Another one that seems to drive a lot of people crazy is that you can't count on the *connectors* that you need will be on the Mac *model* you need. For example, now most Mac models come with FireWire standard, but even a year or more after Apple introduced FireWire, only certain models had it, and if you bought a Mac without doing your research, and just assumed it had FireWire connectors, well, it might not.

Some models have connectors for video projectors, and some don't. It's a connector crapshoot. Why can't all Macs come with the same connectors? That would be too easy (and making the connectors different here and there, is what Apple management does for fun).

What's going to happen:

Someone that really cares about Apple is going to say something about Apple management that really strikes a chord with you, and it will stick with you for years to come.

For example:

I was sitting in the audience for a keynote address by longtime Apple evangelist Guy Kawasaki at the Sunbelt Graphics show in Atlanta back in 1995. The theme of Guy's keynote was taken from his clever and inspiring business book, *How to Drive Your Competition Crazy.* He used some of the great things that Apple had done over the years to "drive its competition crazy," but he let the audience in on how he really felt about Apple when he said this: "Apple management. It's an oxymoron." It stuck with me.

CompUSA: Your own private hell

You can avoid it for as long as possible. You can pretend it doesn't exist, or look the other way when you drive by it, but sooner or later, it's going to come into your life, and it's going to mess you up, but good.

That's right, one day you'll be stressing on an important project for work. As usual, you're on a tight deadline, and sure enough, your printer will start to run out of ink.

Oh, you'll try to hurry and print out the last few pages, but when ink cartridges start to run out, those babies go dry at warp speed, and before you know it, you're faced with a real-life Macintosh dilemma. You can't call a catalog company and have them ship you an ink cartridge overnight—you need to print out this project *today*. You need an ink cartridge right now, and you shudder as you realize that the day has finally come. You're going to have to go back to your local CompUSA store (which you dutifully avoided for nearly a year and a half), because you know that they have the replacement cartridge you need.

Now, why would going to CompUSA be such a traumatic event that many Mac users do their best to avoid it? Is CompUSA a bad store? Are the prices outrageously high? Is their service outrageously bad? Are they just plain mean people? Absolutely not. CompUSA is a great store. That is, unless you're a Mac person. Then it becomes your own personal hell.

It's because CompUSA is the most startling visualization of how incredibly small Apple is in the overall computing world. It's 44,000 square feet of "you can't have this!" and "this isn't for you." But tucked away in the back corner of the store, strategically located as far from the front door as humanly possible—so far away from the cash registers that it's in a different ZIP code, is the "Apple Store within a Store." That is your destiny.

It doesn't hurt to pack a light lunch and wear comfortable shoes, because it's going to take a while to get there. You'll see many fallen comrades along the way. Other Mac users just like you, some still in their Apple T-shirts, sprawled out in the aisles, too exhausted to continue—too humiliated to turn back. Some will be clutching empty ink cartridges, while others will be holding a broken USB cable from their keyboard, but they're just too weak to go on. Sure, you promise to come back to get them, but you never do. At closing time, the assistant managers drag them by their ankles out to the street, where they collect, until their families come back from the shopping mall to pick them up. They'll return to fight, yet another day.

If you reach this "pot of gold at the end of the rainbow," you'll be faced with a harsh reality akin to looking behind the curtain and finding that "the great and powerful Oz" is just some crazy old guy, half in the bag.

In many cases, you'll find that the "Apple Store within a Store" is actually more like the "Apple shelves in the very, very back of a large building." There is little breathable oxygen. It's damp, dimly lit, with abandoned rusted-out cars littering the area, and there's a low-level fog that never seems to lift. (It's not really like that, but it actually might be more fun if it were. Kind of like shopping at the "*Blade Runner* Store within a Store.")

The quality and arrangement of these Apple Store within a Store areas (the brainchild of the "brain child") vary widely from store to store. I have a CompUSA about 10 minutes from my home, and its Apple Store within a Store (from here on out, for the sake of space we'll call it by the acronym ASS) consists of: two sets of shelves for Mac keyboards, mice, connectors, cables, joysticks, and other small peripherals. On each of these freestanding cases is an end cap, and there's a Mac on each, running the appropriate Mac demos, with a Harman/Kardon audio system usually connected to at least one of the two units.

Along the left side wall is a row of iMacs, G4s, and monitors—most of them up and running. On the right wall is a row of large shelves, with Mac software from floor level up to about eight feet high, and the shelves are about 16 or so feet long. Not bad. There's one more shelf up front on the left, and it has some Mac-compatible printers, scanners, and other small peripherals. There's also a few hanging Apple banners and a "Think different" poster or two, so you know that you're actually in the ASS.

So—a few shelves, some Macs, printers, and some Apple posters. That's our ASS. It's not a big ASS, but it's comparable to the size of some of the other ASSes I've seen at other CompUSAs. Of course, I'd love to see a Mac section five times the size of this, but since this ASS concept came to CompUSA, this is the most Mac software and hardware they've ever carried, so I hesitate to complain too loudly. It's important to note that before the ASSes, sales of Apple products represented 2% of CompUSA's total sales. After Steve Jobs brought in his ASS, it jumped up to 15%, so apparently it's working for all parties involved.

I really don't have too many complaints about the ASS itself, because like I said, this is much better than what we had before. My main complaint with the ASS is generally who is manning it (and this has been a constant complaint since it was introduced). If you go into the section, you'll be helped by one of three people:

(1) A real Macintosh person who has been trained by Apple.

(2) An actual Apple employee (this is new, and not available in all stores as of yet, but is reportedly a response to complaints about lack of real Mac people in the ASS).

(3) A drone from the PC department who really wants nothing to do with the ASS, but sees a frustrated customer all alone in the ASS looking for help. So he eventually wanders over to tell him, basically, I'm not the ASS guy, so I can't help you. Come in Thursday because that's when all the ASS guys are here. My only hope is—the PC drone guy isn't using this acronym when talking with customers.

In my past three or four visits there, I've been met by #1 once, and #3 twice. What I'm waiting for is to go there, and actually find #2 in the ASS. (I know, I know, that last one is just *wrong!* I just couldn't help myself.)

The fairy-tale land CompUSA

Over the years, I've had countless letters from frustrated Mac users complaining about their ASS (mostly about staffing problems, limited selection, poor setup and maintenance of the area, or they complain about being approached by PC salesmen hanging out in the ASS who tried to convince them to go over and look at the latest PCs). But I can tell you this—I doubt that Apple will ever respond to these complaints, or have any idea of how far an ASS can fall into decay from lack of interest.

That's because one of the closest CompUSAs to Apple's headquarters (the store in downtown San Francisco, about a block from where Macworld Expo is held) is absolutely unbelievable (and Apple, on some level, probably thinks all CompUSAs are like that). Hell, that store could be called MacUSA and no one would blink an eye. It looks like Apple actually owns that store, and if it were the real model for the ASS nationwide, Apple would have tripled its market share in no time. If anyone from Apple goes into that store, they'll be so busy patting themselves on the back that the very thought of someone criticizing it would be so petty as to be ignored without a second thought.

On the top floor of this "fairy-tale land" CompUSA (oh yes, the Apple presence is on multiple floors), is an area filled with all the latest Macs. It looks something akin to Apple's own trade show booth, with loads of Apple logos on white airy backgrounds. Macs appear on bottom-lit cylindrical pedestals, and elegant displays and "Think different" artwork abounds. It's just flat-out beautiful, and there's lots of cool stuff (and plenty of people were there that morning, playing with Macs—you could hardly move around). No software or peripherals here—just lots of cool Macs!

When you head down the escalator, you're greeted by the Apple Internet Cafe, with free, live, high-speed connections to the Net, and a Mac at every table. On the other side of the escalators is what has to be the largest Mac section of any CompUSA on the planet.

I've got to imagine that either Apple subsidizes this store to some extent, or this CompUSA just sells so much Mac stuff that Apple doesn't need to. But my point is this: If your letter about "The Apple Store within a Store just isn't cutting it" falls on the desk of an Apple employee whose experience at the Apple Store within a Store has been at the downtown San Francisco store, your letter is likely to fall into the trash.

Now, if Steve Jobs visited my local CompUSA, he'd probably take a swing at the manager, but that's probably pretty unlikely. (Steve visiting my local store that is. I think he'd definitely take a swing at the manager.)

It's not the Apple area that bothers us... it's the rest of the store!

Interestingly enough, it's not the Apple Store within a Store that makes CompUSA a Mac user's private hell. Quite the contrary. It's the rest of the store. It's having to walk through tens of thousands of square feet of stuff that you can't have. It's walking through aisle after aisle of games with cool-sounding names, and on-screen weapons you'd love to fire, but when you pick up the box it says "for Win 98, 2000, XP."

It's passing rows of keyboards, mice with two buttons, three buttons, four buttons, and more. It's passing joystick after joystick after joystick (why in the world PC users need so many joysticks is really beyond me). It's passing section after section of toys and gadgets, and loads of crap I really don't need or even want, but just knowing I can't have it makes me want it even more. That's the kind of stuff that turns the store into your own private hell.

It's like getting a job at a Vegas buffet the day you join Weight Watchers. It's like quitting smoking and then getting transferred to Raleigh, North Carolina. It's like trying to give up partying and Rick James moves in next door. IT'S…JUST…NOT…FAIR!

Don't give them ammo

Want to really dip your toe into the bowels of hell? Head on down to your local CompUSA wearing an Apple T-shirt. (For some sick reason, Mac users seem to be drawn to this self-destructive behavior like a mosquito to a bug zapper—I almost always see a Mac fanatic, in full Apple regalia, standing front-and-center near the row of Macs, talking to the ASS man as if to say "this is where I belong!")

When you wear an Apple T-shirt, the PC users already shopping in CompUSA know why you're there (and how little is there for you), and you see in their eyes the delight they take in the whole process as you go hiking by. They give you that look like, "This is all for me. I can have any of it. I am king!" It's as if they want to stop you and say, "Oh look, a cool game—I think I might buy it" or "Wow! That's a cool keyboard—maybe I'll get it, too!" Because they know all too well that even though this might be our private hell, CompUSA is their version of heaven. This is where they momentarily even the score. This is where they thumb their noses at us and symbolically say, "Sure, we spend way more time troubleshooting our machines; and sure we're either tracking down a virus or hanging on hold for tech support; and yes, we spend more time rebooting than you spend working; but now, we're not at our computers. We're out doing what PC users do best—buying stuff *you* can't buy just because we can (in fact, we don't even need, or want, this stuff. We just buy it to exert our PC-buying power)." These are some truly lonely people.

It's not as bad as it first may seem

For many Mac users, going into a CompUSA for the first time can be very unsettling. That's generally why we recommend traveling in groups of three or more. That way, if one of you should become suddenly faint, feels an anxiety attack coming on, or is approached by a salesperson from the PC department, the others will be there to lend the appropriate support. Remember: There's safety in numbers.

Now that you've come this far, I feel I owe you something. I feel you've earned the right to learn an inside secret about CompUSA. You see, things at CompUSA aren't really as bad as they may first seem, and once you learn why, it can help change CompUSA from your own private hell into more of a computer shopping purgatory. That secret is… (insert dramatic sound effect here. Something along the lines of "Bump, bump, ba-dummmmmm") that there is actually lots of Mac software and peripherals available in other parts of the store—you just have to know where to look. Knowing this one simple tip can transform CompUSA from its lowly seven Mac shelves and a "Think different" poster into a Macintosh superstore the likes of which haven't been seen outside of downtown San Francisco.

Here's how I learned the secret. I was at CompUSA one day (yes, buying an ink cartridge), and I was standing in the checkout line waiting to pay. In the area where you wait in line, CompUSA usually has large bins of closeout PC software, mostly games, that they're blowing out for $10. I generally don't waste my time looking through the closeout bin, because it's all PC stuff, but this one day, the line took me so close to the bin that I saw an educational game that I wished I could've bought for my 4 1/2-year-old son. It was *Tonka Construction* and I knew my son would've loved it. I reached over to the game and thought, "Why can't they make stuff like this for the Mac?" and as I looked at the screen shots on the box, I noticed that on the spine it said: "Win 95/98 or Macintosh." "Macintosh!" I yelled. "It says Macintosh!"

I held the box up to show the woman behind me in line. "Look, it says 'Macintosh!' " She looked at me at like "how nice for you," but I didn't care. I found a piece of Mac-compatible software outside the ASS section. So I started digging in the $10 bin. The first seven or eight titles I pulled out were all for Windows, but then I found another Mac game, *Reader Rabbit*. For Macintosh!

Suddenly, I saw CompUSA in a whole new light. I dropped my two software boxes and started running through the store, straight for the children's software section (I had never been in that part of the store before, because after all, I'm a Mac guy, and have thus been relegated to seven shelves just south of Siberia), but as soon as I got there, I picked up a *Star Wars, Episode I* game for kids, and son of a gun—it was for Mac too! I ran up and down the aisles grabbing title after title, even loads of Disney software and it was Mac, Mac, Mac! Before long, I was lying on the floor, covered with boxes of Mac-compatible educational software. As I rolled over, at the end of the aisle I saw another parent lying there (in a tattered Apple T-shirt). He was clutching a copy of *Jump Start Toddlers.* He had obviously been there a while and could barely move, but he raised his head just enough to make eye contact, and he muttered those words I had always longed to hear, "It says it works with Macintosh," and he broke into this huge grin. I could see a tear stream down his face, as the assistant manager dragged him by the ankles out of the store.

He too had uncovered the secret, and seeing his joy gave me an extra burst of energy and I was able to expand my search into the regular games section. Here's what I found—a number of games come on *hybrid disks*—CDs that contain both a Mac and a PC version. All I had to do was keep checking boxes until I found which games were hybrid. This wasn't nearly as much fun in the games department as it was in the children's department, where every other game seemed to be available for Macintosh. In the games area, I would go through at least 20 or 30 games before uncovering a single hybrid. I learned quickly that any game from Microsoft was PC only, so that saved some time; and I didn't find any games from EA Sports that were Mac-compatible, so I stopped looking at those as well.

Again, this gaming search wasn't nearly as fulfilling as my endeavors in the children's area, but at least I did uncover a few gems that I would never have known existed. This was an epiphany. Tons of titles come on hybrid CDs, but CompUSA and all the other retailers display them only in the Windows section. So it *looks* as if there's less Mac software than there really is. Why aren't these titles in *both* sections? It's all part of that "There's no software for Macs" plot.

Then I moved into the hardware area. I was taking a big risk here and I knew it. But then I had another epiphany. Wait just a minute! My Mac has USB connectors, and most of these peripherals are USB! So I started looking and sure enough, some said "Mac-compatible" right on the box. So there I was, smack dab in the middle of the PC peripherals section, looking at stuff I could buy! I looked to my left and there was another shopper looking at a USB hub. She had this pleasant little smile on her face, and that's when I noticed she was holding the software box for Apple's Final Cut Pro (a Mac-only product) under her arm. We looked at each other with that knowing "we've learned the secret" look and both of us started to grin. We hugged, and went our separate ways—never exchanging a spoken word.

I saw her for just a moment on my way to the checkout counter. She was giving sips of water from her canteen to a Mac user sitting on the floor. He was dehydrated, exhausted, leaning against a stack of ViewSonic 21" display cartons, trying to catch his breath. I honestly don't know if he ever made it all the way back to the Apple Store within a Store. Some never do.

On my way to the checkout, I passed a section with speaker systems and subwoofers for PCs. I had seen the Harman/Kardon, clear, iMac subwoofer back in the ASS, but this section, clearly the PC section, had dozens of cool speaker systems. Better yet, they were set up in a console where you could hear different sets of speakers by just pressing a button (kind of like at some stereo stores). The ones I fell in love with were from Altec Lansing, but I knew they were for PC. Then, right beside me, I noticed the salesman from the ASS was picking up a set of speakers and walking back toward the ASS. I said, "Excuse me. Can you use these audio systems with Macs?" He said, "Sure, most of 'em. The connectors are pretty much the same. Make sure you check out the Altec Lansings—I use them myself." I couldn't contain it any longer. I broke into tears. Before I knew it, I was standing at the checkout counter with games for my son, a game for me, a color inkjet printer (with replacement cartridges), a joystick, and an Altec Lansing audio system with a huge beige subwoofer that looked like hell, but sounded like heaven.

CompUSA became a different place for me that day, and now I no longer go out of my way to avoid going there. In fact, every time I visit the nearby Barnes & Noble bookstore, I stroll next door and wander around the entire store. Now every aisle, every section, can uncover another hidden gem, and if I wore the right shoes, ate a hearty breakfast, and got in a good workout that morning, who knows—I might even take a hike back and see what's in the ASS. Life is good.

CHAPTER SEVEN

Why PC users need Apple

I f you really want to learn about how intolerant PC users can be toward Mac users, become an editor of a Macintosh magazine. About once a week, I get an e-mail from a PC user smugly informing me that I might as well give up the fight because Apple is dead and Microsoft has won the war.

The content of these letters is evenly divided between ridiculing what they call "my pointless defense of Apple" and a paragraph or so on how superior PCs are. These e-mails are generally self-congratulatory in tone, as if the writers personally were the victors, rather than Intel, Dell, or Microsoft.

They want us gone!

I've pretty much gotten used to these e-mails, because I've been receiving them for years. But the one thing I really can't understand is their central theme, which is usually "Apple's dead and we're absolutely delighted about it!" To this day, I'm still somewhat surprised that they're so passionate about their desire to see Apple wiped out of existence.

Back in the old days, when I'd get these e-mails, I would craft lengthy replies, dissecting their uninformed arguments line by line (I generally have more ammo at the ready than the 86th Airborne Division).

I'd go into detail countering their claims with real facts and figures about Apple that: (a) they hadn't heard from the PC-biased press and (b) they could not logically refute because, after all, these were facts—complete with references and sources to back them up.

But they'd just respond that what I sent them were lies (regardless of the sources I supplied), and it would just get uglier from there. They'd start cussing, launching personal attacks, calling me names— some would even bring my mother into it—really nasty stuff. I soon realized there was nothing I could say, no fact or figure I could supply that would change their minds and reverse their deep-seated hatred for Apple.

Nowadays, when I get PC-weenie hate mail, I don't go through the whole "dog-and-pony show" of a detailed reply. I just send them back this simple response, "Oh yeah, and you're a big stupid fathead!" That's usually the end of it. I'm fully aware that this sort of sophomoric reply does nothing to help our cause, but it does a lot to keep me out of therapy.

I guess it just amazes me that there are people out there who will interrupt their busy lives to send hate mail to the editor of a magazine that deals with a product they don't use.

I could understand being mad at or frustrated with Apple if you're an Apple customer (in fact, that's a special part of the overall Macintosh experience), but if you don't use their product—really, why would you *care?*

For example, when I'm on the road I often rent cars from National rent-a-car. I like National, and as a National customer I've been peeved at them on occasion over stuff like losing my reservation or not having the car available that I reserved. But even though I'm a pretty solid National customer, I have no passionate interest in seeing Avis or Hertz go out of business. I just don't care. In fact, I like the price and service competition that Avis and Hertz bring to the rental car business.

So what's with these people who send me the nasty e-mails? How would it enhance their lives if Apple went belly up? I guess that as much as we can't understand why they hate Apple so much, they probably can't understand why we feel about Apple the way we do. So I thought I'd examine why Mac users care about Apple in an effort to help the haters see the light, and the error in their death wish for Apple. The most ironic part of it all is that Apple's continued success is especially important to PC users. They just don't know it. Yet.

So who are the innovators?

Let's look at PC industry leader, Compaq. They're known for assembling well-built computers. Good looks, good construction, an Intel chip inside. But Apple, on the other hand, is a technology company. Frankly, comparing Apple to Compaq isn't really fair. It isn't fair to Compaq, because they're just a hardware company, whereas Apple is both a hardware and a software company.

But what really makes Apple so special is that Apple *creates.* Apple *invents.* Apple *innovates.* You can see Apple's innovations in many of Compaq's own products. For example, next time you're in CompUSA, take a look at their PC laptops. You'll notice that almost every laptop has a trackpad, rather than a trackball or a mouse. That's Apple technology. Apple was the company that introduced the trackpad to laptop computing and now it's the standard for both PCs and Macs. If it weren't for Apple, we'd still be using those lame trackballs.

While you're there, slide on down to the section where they have the desktop PCs. CD-ROM drives are standard on about every machine, right? Have been for years, right? That's because Apple changed the industry by being the first company to introduce a personal computer with a built-in CD-ROM drive.

Also, take a look at how many PCs no longer offer floppy disk drives. Why, after all these years of including floppy disk drives, are some PC manufacturers no longer including them in their units? It's because Apple did it first. That's right, when Apple introduced the iMac, it was the first personal computer to do away with the floppy drive, and it was a very controversial move. Apple then did away with floppy drives on all Macs across the board. The PC industry laughed at the idea—until they realized that once again Apple was leading the way—and now even they have started remov-ing their floppy drives. By the way (and this may sound weird at first), it was Apple who originally introduced the first personal computer with a floppy disk drive, and they were the first to use the smaller 3-1/2" disk drive that is still in use in many PCs today. So in essence, Macintosh was the first personal computer to ship

with a floppy disk drive, and the first personal computer to ship
without one. Both were gutsy moves—stuff you'd expect from the
industry innovator.

Now stroll over to the printer aisle. You'll notice that nearly every
PC printer touts its use of TrueType fonts. They probably don't
mention on the box that the font technology's full name is *Apple
TrueType*. That's right, the standard for font technology on the PC
was created by Apple. It was created originally to compete with
Adobe PostScript Type 1 fonts (Apple had been licensing PostScript
fonts from Adobe for their laser printer line), and the added benefit
of TrueType was that you didn't need Adobe Type Manager (ATM)
to smooth the type on screen. However, it failed to supplant the huge
already installed base of Adobe Type 1 font users. So what do you
do with Apple technology that wasn't adopted by the professional
market? Get Microsoft to adopt it and push it on the PC crowd—
where it's still the standard today.

Apple's list of innovations is impressive by any standard, and
many of the ideas, technologies, and peripherals PC users take for
granted today were either invented by Apple or Apple was the first
to include the invention in their products.

For example, Apple was the first to offer a personal computer
with color graphics when they introduced the Apple II. Apple was
the first to offer built-in networking, and more recently the first to
offer built-in wireless local area networking (and the first to offer
dual built-in antennas as well). Macs were the first computers to
offer built-in sound, something that is standard in today's PCs; but
until just a few years ago, many PC users had to buy and install a
separate sound card.

Apple was the first computer company to provide easy access to the inside of the computer via a screwless latch (this is a bigger deal than it first sounds, because it took quite an innovative design to make the guts of the computer and the motherboard so easily accessible). Incidentally, other PC manufacturers, such as Dell are now starting to introduce models with this type of easy access.

Macs were the first computers to offer the ability to connect more than one monitor (a capability Macs had for years, but wasn't introduced on the PC until Windows 98).

Apple was the company that invented the PDA (Personal Digital Assistant) with its hand-held Newton which, like the PDAs of today, featured built-in handwriting recognition (okay, admittedly, it barely recognized anyone's handwriting, but that's not to say it didn't try). Although the Newton was as popular as the XFL football league, it still was the first hand-held PDA and it helped open the door to what has become a huge PDA market.

More gutsy, industry-leading moves still come from Apple today. For example, Apple was the first company to make USB connectors standard across its entire line (now nearly all PCs use USB). Amusingly, the USB standard was developed in the PC world, but nobody used it until Apple did—and pushed the entire industry to move forward. Then came FireWire: an Apple invention that is now universal among PCs. All the connectivity wonders of FireWire devices—digital cameras, camcorders, drives of all kinds—are Apple's gift to PC users.

Apple was the first company to offer all LCD flat-panel displays and do away with its tube-based models. Others will follow. Also,

Apple was the first company to do away with noisy internal fans (in the iMac and Cube) by creating designs that can self-cool by convecting hot air out of the computer case. Others in the industry are already starting to follow Apple's lead. Again.

This is just the beginning of what makes Apple truly special among the computer companies of the world. It offers you some insight as to why we care, and why PC users should care as well. Apple doesn't just assemble computer boxes; it leads, transforms, and shapes an entire industry—and both Mac users and PC users benefit from their vision.

If your PC looks good, thank Apple too!

If there's anything PC users should be thankful to Apple for, it is that their PCs probably aren't as ugly as they used to be. That's because Apple brought the computer's looks to the forefront, and made PC manufacturers step back, take a look at the square beige boxes they were offering, and try to create something better.

It was Apple's innovation that transformed the entire computing market again when it introduced the iMac, and then again when it offered them in the customer's choice of five different colors. This industry awakening, which happened back in the late 1990s, not only radically changed the computing market, it also had a major effect on the entire consumer market. Shortly after the five different-colored iMacs were introduced, everything from vacuum cleaners to hamburger grills tried to emulate the success of the iMac by offering products in similar translucent colors. (When I saw fine Swiss watchmaker Rolex introduce iMac-influenced watches with translucent plastic in different colors, I took this as a clear sign of the coming apocalypse.)

After the success of the iMacs, PC manufacturers raced to add some translucent-colored plastic to their units—as if that alone would transform an otherwise boring beige box into an iMac. It didn't work—not a single manufacturer had a home run with any of their iMac "me too!" models, and now most PC manufacturers have returned to what they do best—basic beige. But now you can tell that PC manufacturers are at least trying to make better-looking computers, and the style of a computer has become important to the computer-buying public. PC users can thank Apple for that, too.

Oh, but there's more...

Another reason we care is simply that Mac users have been spoiled by Apple. We've always gotten the hottest technology first. From simple stuff, such as icons, folders, pull-down menus (which appeared on the Mac OS when the PC world was still using DOS. How do you think they wound up in the first shipping version of Windows—coincidence?), to more advanced technology like CD-ROMs, trackpads, FireWire, etc.

Mac users are also spoiled by always having the hottest software first. Applications, such as Adobe Photoshop, Painter, PageMaker, QuarkXPress, Adobe GoLive, Adobe Illustrator, and even business applications, such as Microsoft Excel and Microsoft Word, were developed for the Macintosh first. Windows versions were introduced later, in some cases many years later. That's another reason why Macintosh is considered the platform of true innovation.

It's not the box. It's what the box does.

Quick, think of an innovation that PC manufacturer Gateway has pioneered that changed the face of computing. Gotcha! There's no arguing, for example, that Compaq makes a decent machine; but if they went out of business tomorrow, the public would just shrug their shoulders and stroll over to a different aisle in CompUSA to buy a Sony, or a Gateway, or an HP that does EXACTLY THE SAME THING. If Compaq dies (or merges with a large printer company), you just buy a different brand. But if Apple dies, the technological leader in personal computing dies along with it.

New inventions would be stifled, new technologies snuffed out, and the only other choice for the technology-hungry public comes from a company that's not best known for original ideas and technology breakthroughs. It's best known for its marketing, amid accusations of cutthroat monopolistic predatory practices and a lengthy investigation by the U.S. Justice department into its trade practices—Microsoft.

The sincerest form of flattery

Microsoft is a marketing juggernaut. It's known as a powerhouse, a monopoly, a company to be feared; but it's not generally known as a real innovator. It's a follower—somebody else has to lead the way.

For example, Netscape had the first Web browser to gain wide acceptance, and it was a huge hit. After being criticized for its lack of Internet initiative, Microsoft quickly licensed the Mosaic technology from Spyglass for a one-time fee and before you know it, Microsoft's Internet Explorer appeared.

AOL and CompuServe had the first online services. Years later Microsoft has MSN.

CNN had the first 24-hour news station; years later Microsoft has MSNBC.

Sony and Phillips had the first TV-based Web browser. Now Microsoft owns WebTV.

Macintosh had a trash can on its desktop for deleting files; 11 years later Microsoft introduced a recycling bin on its desktop for deleting files.

Apple developed iMovie, a simple and incredibly innovative software package that made editing digital video easy for anyone.

When Microsoft introduced Windows XP, it too came with a free digital video-editing software package called, "Windows Movie Maker." Every time I see it on it TV, all I can think of is, "Gee, that looks a lot like iMovie."

Speaking of Windows XP (which was introduced after Mac OS X, just like Windows 95 was introduced after Mac OS 8, and Windows 2000 was introduced after Mac OS 9), the first time I saw it, once again I thought, "Gee, that looks awfully familiar."

If somebody else can come up with an original idea, Microsoft can find a way to make a buck with it—even if the product they produce isn't nearly as good. And I'm not alone in this opinion. In fact, Larry Elisson, CEO of Oracle (the second-largest software company in the world), in a 1998 interview with PC Week Online said, "Microsoft has innovated nothing. The thing I find most contemptible is Bill's lying, this thing about innovating. It makes me want to puke. That's innovation a la Rockefeller, not innovation a la Edison."

So why do we care so much?

We care because we realize that Apple's not just another company, it's much more human than that. It has vision, creativity, it has a sense of humor, a conscious and genuine desire to create something better. This attracts a certain kind of customer. A devoted customer. A passionate customer. One who deeply understands firsthand how different computing would be without it.

There's an intrinsic value to owning a Macintosh, a certain connection between you and the machine, similar to the connection Porsche owners feel with their sports cars, Harley Davidson owners feel about their motorcycles, Krispy Kreme customers feel about their donuts, that you just can't put down on paper.

It's the fear of giving up that feeling—of lowering your standards to settle for something less—that sends chills up the spines of Macintosh users. That's why Macintosh users have a genuine desire that Apple makes it. Maybe that's why we care the way we do. But even though most PC users don't "get it," luckily we do.

That's why with all the Apple-bashing, Microsoft bias, bad news in the press, and an 18-year all-out assault on Apple, the company just posted another quarterly profit in the millions, and still has billions in the bank. Apple will sell millions of Macintosh computers this year to devoted, creative people who do "get it;" people who do care about owning something special, and therefore, care about the company that makes it—Apple Computer.

CHAPTER EIGHT

"Don't pick fights with people who buy ink by the barrel"

—LYNDON B. JOHNSON

I mentioned in the previous chapter that I get a steady stream of e-mails from PC users who are taking issue with the whole Mac versus PC thing, and how we've "lost the war." They want to engage in some light-to-medium e-mail sparring, but I've pretty much lost my enthusiasm for that sort of engagement (I'm over it), so I pretty much just let it roll off my back.

But there is one type of letter that I just can't resist. A letter so delightful that when I get one, I have to call everyone into my office and read it aloud. The kind of "Letter to the Editor" that makes it all worthwhile to take all the crap an editor of a Macintosh magazine gets. Specifically, it's any letter from an angry PC user that starts with "I dare you to print this letter." How could seven little words sound any sweeter? For what this poor soul has just done is to put into motion a public plea for e-mail suicide. They've guaranteed that if their letter is printed (and believe me, it will be), we'll go to great lengths to ensure that the person who wrote it will perhaps appear to be the most ignorant person that ever lived.

Anytime someone sends us a "nasty-gram," as a courtesy they are instantly pre-approved for a humiliating, all-out, public slam-fest (the act which is referred to in our offices as "Shooting them out of a cannon"). Getting these types of letters creates a sense of purpose among our ranks, an esprit de corps that ripples throughout the office, and after reading each letter aloud (and bursting into laughter at nearly every sentence), to celebrate we usually close up early and go to the park for ice cream. This is what it's all about. Nuking some poor slob who just doesn't know any better than "to pick fights with people who buy ink by the barrel."

What we love about this (and what they must not realize) is that if they send us a nasty-gram, we publicly nuke them back to the Stone Age, right there in print (and on the Web) for everyone to read and laugh along, and that's the end of it. They don't get to respond in print, because we don't have to let them. Is that a bit unfair? Absolutely! Just like life.

Second place is good, too.
The important thing is...you tried your best

So, if getting a letter from an irate PC user is about as much fun as we can stand, what's in second place? This letter is so eagerly anticipated, it's almost tied for first—a letter from a PC user pretending to be a Mac user. We absolutely love these! They pretend to be Mac users so that we'll print their anti-Mac letter, and then, "Boy, won't we feel stupid." Now, how do we know these letters are from PC users pretending to be Mac users? What if they're real letters from concerned Macintosh users who, like you, want to tackle some real issues and have constructive criticisms for Apple? Fat chance. These goobers give away their cover in about two sentences.

Typical mistakes include constantly capitalizing the word Mac as MAC (a dead giveaway in uncovering fake PC losers). Another popular "tell" is when they start their letters something like this:

"I use an Apple, just like you. I love my Apple computer. But aren't you concerned that PCs are cheaper, and there's not much software for Apple? Why, I can buy a Micron 1200-MHz PC, with 500 MB of RAM, blah, blah, blah…"

So what's wrong with their letters? First off, Macintosh users don't call their computer an "Apple computer." They call it a Mac, or a Macintosh. Apple is the company that makes it. For example, if you own a Chrysler New Yorker, and you're talking about your car, you don't refer to it is a "Chrysler car." You call it a New Yorker, or a Chrysler New Yorker. Not a Chrysler car. So calling it "an Apple computer" is a definite "tell."

Another giveaway is that they know the make, model, and specs of a PC and quote them in their letters. Mac users don't care about PCs, don't know their specs, and certainly don't quote them in letters to Macintosh magazines. But the trait that's common to all "fake Mac user" letters is that they quickly get past the "I love Macs, but…" so they can get to the real reason they wrote—to use the same outdated, boring, heard-it-a-million-times attacks that uninformed PC users everywhere use when bashing Apple and the Macintosh platform. Their letters drone on and on about the lack of Mac software and cheaper PCs; they lament the fact that you can't "customize your Apple computer" by adding a new video card (as if that weren't a giveaway in itself); and more of the same outdated crap we've heard for years.

I guess what they think is "Hey, if I pretend to be a Macintosh user, then they'll print my anti-Mac letter and all their readers will finally hear the truth, about how bad the Mac platform really is, with all its shortcomings, and all their readers will switch to PCs." I mean seriously, what do they hope to achieve? Even better yet, why are they reading a Macintosh magazine in the first place? To keep track of what "the other side" is doing? Honestly, what is their motivation? Better yet, when they write these letters (the angry PC ones at least), what do they expect the outcome to be? Do they think our official reply is going to be "Dear PC user: Ya know, I think you may be onto something here. You're right—there's not enough software, I can't install a new video card, and our Macs cost too much. You've convinced us and we're changing the foundation this magazine was built upon; and we are now officially recommending to our readers that they switch to PC and buy the 1200-MHz Micron with the Intel chip!"

If that's what they were hoping for, boy were they surprised when they read our "Letters to the Editor" page in the next issue.

The real thing!

Now that I'm editing *Mac Design Magazine,* our PC bash-fest has really subsided, because we just don't have the space to do the PC slamming we like to do (because of all the graphics tutorials) so we pretty much limit our PC bashing to two areas in the magazine: the letters page and the table of contents. A little bit sneaks into the news section, but nothing like we did in the old days.

One reason we lightened up on the PC bashing is that Apple's fortunes have improved so much that we don't need to do it like we did when the whole world was piling up against us every day. Things are better, Apple is better, and it really takes the edge off the need to bash like we used to.

However, to this day, the letters column is still one of the most popular segments in the magazine, and we still get letters every week from readers who tell us, "The first thing I read every issue is your letters page, to hear you blast some hapless PC user."

I have to admit, writing the responses is actually a lot of fun, because it's the one time I can let my manners go out the window. I can say the things that I really want to say, and not worry about offending the writers, because I don't want them for readers anyway (after all, they're PC users and we're a Mac magazine). So when a letter like that comes in, I simply "load the cannons!"

I can go on telling you about their ridiculous letters, and our "take-no-prisoners" responses, but really I thought that you'd enjoy reading actual letters and the responses that we printed in the magazine over the years (in *Mac Today* and now, in *Mac Design Magazine*). That's the only way you'll get a real feel for the kind of people we're dealing with. Plus, as an added benefit, you get to sit back and enjoy the public flogging they received for all their efforts.

Now, what you're about to read are excerpts from letters to the editor and my responses, but because we've already nuked these poor bastards once, and because we follow a "double-jeopardy" rule of not nuking a PC loser a second time, I'll withhold the real name and e-mail address of the PC weenie in question (both of which appeared in the printed magazines). That way, they won't lose their jobs, their car, and any dignity they might have had left after their friends and family saw their letter in print. Also, I will run a few letters that are just so plain stupid that they didn't need a rebuttal. Here goes…

Let the bashing begin!

In the letter of the month, you slam a PC user who wrote in to you. Assuming for the sake of argument that he was misguided, why would you honor one irrational letter by printing it just to slam it?

Second, the "logical rebuttal" (just to make sure you idiots understand, I'm being sarcastic) represents the writer's letter as "defending the PC." He is not! He is promoting the virtues of knowing your machine. Know your place and show some humility!

I realize that there might be holes in the letter above but my time is valuable. I've got other things to do. Nonetheless, I'll expect civil treatment of the substance of my message, not some grade school jabs covered with the "kidding" claim.

When you have less talk and more walk (that means substance), you'll have my paid subscription and respect (or is this magazine a not-for-profit thing?).

WILLIAM SNOTTYBRITCHES
(Not his real name, but if it was, who could argue?)

[The Editor responds] Dear William:
You're lucky you wrote to us, because we're really nice people. But I have to warn you, there are a lot of magazines out there that, when you write in and call them "idiots," tell them to "know their place," expound on how "valuable your time is," and dangle your "do what I want and then you'll have my paid subscription" crap, they would respond by saying, "Who the hell do you think you are, you little snot? We don't want your stinkin' subscription, in fact we don't want you as a reader, and generally we think you're just another angry loser with nothing better to do with his life than write nasty letters," but I just want you to know, we would never do that. By the way, even though you called us "idiots" we don't think you're one (kidding!).

The reason Apple is going into the toilet is because you guys just don't get it. You're more worried about the propaganda than you are about the realities.

See ya in Amiga, Atari, & TRS 80 land.

NAME WITHHELD
(Because he was a dumb ass)

The thing I really can't wait for is the time when Macs really take off. If Mac sells more computers…the price of PCs will also go down. The sad thing is, a decent Mac system will probably still cost $5,000. Are you a Mac user…oh. Sorry!"

GASIUS CHESEMAKER
(Hopefully, not his real name)

[The Editor responds] Dear Gasius:
*First, before I answer your letter, it's Apple; if **Apple** sells more comput-ers, goober! Now, "if PCs get cheaper you get your system, support, and software for next to nothing." That's good, because using a PC you're definitely going to need some tech support, and as for getting it for next to nothing—it's like they always say—you get what you pay for.*

Gees! Why does this stuff matter so much to you guys? Don't you understand that when you make fun of PC users, insinuating that they are all blithering cretins whose highest form of literary compo-sition is bashing Mac users, all you are doing is invalidating your claim of having risen above it all.

You can go on and on about how PC users "don't get it," it being the reason for using a Macintosh, but looking at the letters presented in your "Letters to the Editor" section, can you really say you understand any better the reason why people choose to use a PC?

This is a forum for discussing Macintosh-related items. Perhaps it is just an intellectual deficiency on my part, but I fail to see how discussing how dumb PC users are adds to this topic.

I guess that's about all I have to say. If this is printed, I guess I'll have some manner of snide comment to look forward to.

Ah well.

OXNARD DROLL

(Not his real name, but probably should be)

[The Editor responds] Dear Oxnard:

Good news—your wait is over! However, you're going to have to wait a little bit longer, because although you secretly want me to call you an insolent, moronic, close-minded bonebutt—I'm not going to do it. That's because everything you said is absolutely true. Your letter has inspired me, and I think I'm going to change the entire editorial focus to provide a more balanced, open-minded, and fair look at both sides of the issues, because that's obviously what the majority of our readers, readers like yourself, are clamoring for. Instead, we'll now focus on trying to appease humorless people who don't use Macintosh at all, and see if we can get them to stop what they're doing and write complaint letters to magazines that address a subject that is of no interest to them whatsoever. You must feel great knowing your letter really made a difference.

I recently read an article where Apple claims speeds over 50% faster than an 800-MHz Pentium III on Photoshop. That sounds cool, but is completely contradictory to an article in the June/July issue of *Popular Mechanics*. They tested several 800-MHz Pentium III machines and Power Mac G4/450s and ran time tests on all. The Mac lost all the tests—by a long shot—except it placed third on ripping MP3 files.

If we are real Mac fans, let's help clear this up.

FAKE MAC GUY
(Surprisingly, that is his real name.)

[The Editor responds] Dear Fake Mac Guy:
Did someone tell you that Popular Mechanics *was a computer maga-*
zine? By the way, if you think that's bad, don't look at Good
Housekeeping's *G4 versus Pentium III speed tests. They make* Sports
Illustrated's *G4/Pentium speed tests look even more off the mark.*

I may be a PC user, but I love Macs too. I just can't afford a decent one. While I could get an iMac for a decent price, it's not much computer. I don't care how fast it is; I am not paying more for the same thing just so I can have pretty plastic colors, and the all-in-one design is just stupid.

Don't get me wrong, I'd love to have a Mac, but...[interrupted by Editor]

SIMON JOLLYBOTTOM
(Hey, that could be his name. You never know.)

[The Editor responds] Dear Simon:
I'm sorry I had to step in and stop your letter, but I don't think even the PC users who read our magazine believe your "I'd love to have a Mac" bull.

I have absolutely no intention of putting up with your magazine.

I make a substantial amount of my income from freelance graphic illustrations, and I do not have the time to waste reading the drivel that you are publishing. Your review of Photoshop 6.0 raved about new features the reviewer thought would be important. I have other programs that can do what Photoshop 6.0 is just now doing.

FUSSI BUCKIT
(His boarding school nickname)

[The Editor responds] Dear Dr. Fussi:
Wait! Give us another chance. We can change. You're right, we should forget about Photoshop and its stupid overrated features. We really want to write about PaintShop Pro for the PC and hear more about the "substantial amount of income" you make with it. We don't want to publish drivel, instead we want fun guys like you to become our readers. Guys that don't have time for drivel, but yet somehow manage to find time to write nasty letters to magazines that don't interest them.

First off, you say that even the most anal-retentive PC user would have to acknowledge that Macintosh computers are easier to set up and use. While this might be partially true, most PCs are equally easy to set up and use. Even if you can get a Mac up and running faster…[interrupted by Editor].

MAJOR DUMASS
(Now that *sounds made up)*

[The Editor responds] Dear Major:
Yeah, yeah. PCs are easy to use, faster than Macs, and never crash.
Next!

Your letters column is the first thing I read every issue. I especially love reading letters from PC owners. It's like watching a slapstick movie. You know the character is stupid, and is about to do something dumb, but it still makes us laugh.

Should we enlighten them with the facts? Absolutely not! We could lose a terrific form of entertainment. Reading about PC users is one of the enormous joys of using a Mac.

ANDREW COOLGUY
(Should be his name, if it isn't)

As an avid Mac user myself, I understand these issues. However, I work in a mixed environment, and I have found that practically anything that you do on a Mac can be done on a PC. I love my Mac, but it's a nagging issue: PC or Mac? The real issue is Apple's backing themselves in to a corner.

Every day I ask myself, "How much longer am I going to continue to dump money into my Mac?"

Your article lists a variety of technologies pioneered on the Mac. Once again, I use both, however…[interrupted by Editor]

ARCHIBALD STUFFYBUT
(I wish his parents really had been named Stuffybut, for obvious reasons.)

[The Editor responds] Dear Arch:
No need to go any further with your letter because, congratulations!
You've just won our award for "PC Weenie pretending to be a Mac user
to make their stupid 'PCs are better' point." You must be very proud.
We'll spare our readers the rest of your annoying letter, which includes a
line-by-line rebuttal of our article where you tell us all how the PC
matches or betters the Mac in every case. It was really nicely done. No
really, it was great. Thanks for playing.

It is unfortunate that you spend so much time and energy insulting users of Wintel systems.

Could it be a lack of new material that forces you to devote so much space to your slamming users of other systems? Get the collective chip set off your shoulders.

FATTHED BONNEBUTTE
(I think that's French.)

[The Editor responds] Dear Fatthed:
Guess what? It's time for us to waste more time and energy. I was going to let you live, but that "collective chip set" PC-geek-speak put me over the edge.
    I can see that you're curious about why we slam PC users. Is it because (a) we can't come up with enough new material, or (b) is it because smug, arrogant PC users insist on writing angry complaint letters to a magazine that covers a product they themselves don't even use? Hmmmm. This is a tough one. Want to phone a friend? How about 50/50? Better yet, let's poll our audience.

First let me point out a few things: While there are many poor quality PCs and PC parts out there, there are PC parts and systems that will match the quality of any ever installed in a Macintosh. While I agree that Macs are well-made machines, I don't think…[interrupted by Editor]

FARQUAR BUTMUNCH
(How sad that's not his real name. Sad. It really suits him.)

[The Editor responds] *Dear Farquar:*
Sorry to cut you off, but you're boring me. Next!

I've just seen your magazine today for the first time. I was disappointed by your lack of objectivity about PCs and Macs.

Why can't you get off your hobby horse and acknowledge that both platforms in this day and age are very similar and have equal merit?

The Mac is strong enough to stand on its own merits, so why don't you dedicate all your editorial work to that, without mocking users of other platforms. Then maybe I will find your magazine has more credibility.

SUMTHINSCOT INMYAS
(A clearly appropriate pseudonym)

[The Editor responds] Dear Sumthinscot:
We sit up at night wondering, "What can we do to make our magazine have more credibility with smug humorless PC users?"

Think before you talk, please! I was disappointed to read your response to a gentleman in your last issue who was inquiring as to why he should buy a Mac over a PC. I concluded after reading these responses that this magazine is run by what we call "Mac Bigots."

I would have answered this man's questions (about how much more stuff you seem to get with a PC purchase as opposed to a Mac) with some facts designed to change his mind. You are doing the Mac community more damage than good when you respond so hostilely to inquiries such as that, and you do nothing to inspire Apple towards greater feats or advances by forgiving their every mistake.

BEEG KNOWITAWL
(It fits.)

[The Editor responds] Dear Beeg:
I went back and reread the letter you're referring to, and I recommend you do the same. When you reread it, I'm sure you'll find that the author of the letter was NOT asking a question, he was making a statement "Why should I [anyone] buy a Mac when PCs are cheaper?" It wasn't a legitimate request for information, and the whole point of his letter was to refute Apple's claims that the G3 chip is faster than Intel's Pentium II. He writes things like, "The iMac isn't as good as you believe" and "The iMac is more expensive than a PC with the same capabilities." He wasn't looking for guidance, he was expressing his (a PC user's) opinion.

But, Beeg, I encourage you to try this: Why don't you drop him an e-mail with reasons why he should choose Macintosh over a PC. If you think our response to those PC users was (as you put it) "disappointing," wait until you get his response.

Obviously, this is the first time you've read an issue of our magazine (it probably caught your eye while you were reaching for that copy of PC Computing), because if it wasn't, you would have already known that (a) we roast all weenies, (b) we are totally biased, we admit it up front, and make no excuses for it, and (c) we love Apple, and because we do we have been very vocal critics of Apple's lame-o advertising for years (at least until Steve came back, hired TBWA/Chiat Day, and fixed everything).

I'm a PC user. Now before you cast me aside as some idiot with nothing better to do than write letters, hear me out. I don't hate Macs. I like them. Why don't I switch then you ask?

There are two (three actually, I hate the one-button mouse) reasons you see; the first is I can't afford it. You can get a 1-GHz PC for under $1,000. A G4 costs more than $1,650. The second reason is compatibility. I'm not a graphic designer, but I am a gamer and most games don't run on Macs. If they do, the Mac version comes out weeks or months later, and...[interrupted by Editor].

IMA IDDIEIT
(*The truth hurts.*)

Dear Ima:
I let you go on longer than the average weenie, probably longer than I should have (especially after your "I'm a gamer" admission), but finally I had to pull the plug. I'm sure you understand.

I feel sorry for people who feel like they have to buy a Mac to do the job at twice the price.

I already know that MACheads refuse to accept the truth. Soooo, don't feel obligated to print the truth, it would only hurt your circulation numbers. Just delete this e-mail now, before anyone sees it.

ALAN STANKBRETH
(He needs an Altoid.)

[The Editor responds] Dear Alan:
Good news! We're not going to call you a stupid loser or make you look really silly for writing in. That's all. Have a great day!

Although your magazine is specifically written for Mac designers, I'm able to make good use of it even though I use an IBM compatible.

I wish I had a Mac but I don't have the funds right now to buy a new computer. I was wondering if you knew of any magazine that dealt with design issues from a PC user's standpoint.

FRED SEEMSOK
(I let him live because, after all, he seems OK.)

[The Editor responds] Dear Fred:
There's a reason that out of the dozens and dozens of PC magazines, there's not even one that deals with design issues from a PC user's standpoint. There's just not enough of an audience. If there were, believe me, with the size of the PC market, it could support ten PC design magazines—but as you pointed out, there are none. So why are all the design magazines focused on Macintosh users? At the risk of sounding smug, why do you think?

It's no doubt that with multimedia, the Macintosh is a force to be reckoned with. However, as a PC user I feel that I have a right to bash Macintosh users, like you immaturely trash Microsoft and PC users.

If you guys are going to rag on Windows users, I could care less, but why don't you present some sound arguments. Cheap shots and needless arguments and insults to Windows and PC users sure won't win them over to a Mac. Certainly Apple wouldn't use this as an advertisement tactic. Or would they?

ARNOLD POOPIEDIEPEE
(His real name when he was on Rugrats)

[The Editor responds] Dear Arnold:
First off, our magazine is NOT a computer magazine. It's a Macintosh magazine, designed expressly for Macintosh users. It's not our job to "win over" Windows users to the Macintosh side—that's Apple's job. Our job is to report Mac news, and teach Macintosh techniques to people who already own one. But we do want to thank you for taking the time to write in and tell us how you, a PC user, think our Macintosh magazine should be written.

How does it make you feel when you are talking in a computer discussion, and you have to turn your head, because people are snickering about you and your Macinturd?

IMAN ASBAG
(If the shoe fits)

[The Editor responds] Dear Iman:
How does it feel when hundreds of thousands of people read your dumbass letter, shake their heads, and think you're an idiot?

Pot shots at Microsoft, the media, and anything else that gets in our way

I've got to believe that on some level, all Mac users secretly hate Microsoft. Okay, some aren't so secret about it (many Mac users refuse to have any Microsoft product installed on their machines, as a show of defiance). And actually "hate" may be too strong a word to describe how all Mac users feel—they don't *all* hate Microsoft. In fact, I've heard there are two sisters somewhere in Montana that don't hate Microsoft, and I've heard tales of a Mac user in Brussels who describes his feelings about Microsoft as "ambivalent," so that's at least three people I can think of right off the top of my head. So saying "all" Mac users hate Microsoft is obviously an exaggeration of sorts (but one that's certainly easy and fun to make).

Now, do I hate Microsoft? Before I answer that question, I need to ask all of Microsoft's attorneys to leave the room (they're everywhere, ya know. Kind of like the CIA). Okay, are they all gone? Good. Now, lean in closer. Here's a little insight: Mac users see Microsoft as two separate companies: (1) a good Microsoft. One that makes great software for the Macintosh, like Microsoft Office, Microsoft Internet Explorer, Outlook Express, etc. and (2) an evil Darth Vader-like Microsoft that makes Windows and 50 million other things only for PC users (like Microsoft Flight Simulator. I know, let it go).

Mac people really do like the Macintosh side of Microsoft. It's run by real Mac people—dedicated Mac heads (like you and me), and their goal is to bring some great software to the Mac platform. That's probably why some of Microsoft's Mac products have features that aren't available on their Windows counterparts. So, for the rest of this book, when I mention Microsoft, I'm not talking about the "good Microsoft" (the Macintosh Business Unit of Microsoft). I'm talking about the other part. The part full of meanies.

But it's not only Mac users that hate Microsoft. I know loads of PC users who absolutely hate Microsoft too. In fact, I can't say for sure that I personally know a PC user who says he/she actually likes Microsoft. They may not hate them, but I haven't found a PC user that likes them, cares about them, etc.

Not that they don't like a particular software program Microsoft makes. They may even like Windows (hey, I've heard stories), but I'm talking about Microsoft the company, not the software. Now, I could be off about this (yeah, right) so try my theory out for yourself: Ask a few PC users you know, "Do you like Microsoft as a company?" and see what they say. See if you get an answer like, "Microsoft—they're great. I'm one of their biggest fans."

Also, you'll probably uncover another difference between Mac users and PC users: Mac users may not like Microsoft, but generally they don't care one way or the other about Bill Gates. However, PC users seem to really have it in for Bill. They're always going off on Bill, and you can tell they just don't like the guy (even if they do use lots of his company's software).

I have a theory on why Bill really fries their hash browns. My theory is that the average Windows user is, on some level, unhappy (not PC experts who troubleshoot their own machines; I'm talking about "the average user"). They feel like "Hey, we're using the right stuff—the same stuff everybody else is using. But we've got all these problems. It's not supposed to be like this, right?" They're unhappy with their overall computing experience (and they're probably unhappy with their hairstyle, clothes, and generally dweeby appearance, but that's another story). But they're not going to blame Dell, or Intel, or the company that makes their monitor—all of that stuff seems to work. Besides, they don't want to blame a big faceless corporation, because they feel this is *someone's* fault. It has to be—it's too messed up, complicated, and unwieldy to have been created by a machine—someone must be behind this. They need to blame a real livin', breathing person for their misery—and who better than the man they themselves helped to make the richest billionaire in the world—Bill Gates? Hey, it's just a theory, but if you have a couple of drinks and read it again, it starts to sound more and more plausible.

So what's the real reason Mac people hate Microsoft? In my opinion, it's because they feel that Microsoft ripped Apple off. By that I mean that Apple was the company to bring icons, pull-down menus, folders, the little trash can, "point-and-click" using a mouse—in short, the whole "Graphical User Interface" to computing. They didn't necessarily invent every piece of it themselves, but Apple is the company that brought it to personal computing, at a time when PC users were using the best OS Microsoft had come up with to that point—DOS. PC users had no icons. No folders. No windows. No mouse! If you wanted a computing environment that offered those things, you had to buy a Macintosh.

A short time after the original Mac was introduced, Microsoft introduced the Windows operating system. Surprisingly enough, it too had icons, pull-down menus, folders, "point-and-click" using a mouse—in short, a "Graphical User Interface." We felt it was a pretty lame knockoff of the Mac OS, so at first we didn't sweat it (although Apple apparently did, and tried to sue Microsoft for a "look-and-feel" infringement). Subsequent versions of Windows added other "Mac-like" features, such as a recycling bin positioned approximately in the same spot that Apple's trash can had occupied for many years. In some cases, Microsoft didn't even change the name of the feature "inspired" by the Mac OS. You know what Microsoft calls their version of the Mac's Control Panels? "The Control Panel." Apple had the "Apple menu," Microsoft introduced the "Start" menu. They both pretty much do the same thing. This is the stuff that burns our biscuits.

But what really scrambles our eggs is that so many PC users wholeheartedly believe to this day, that Microsoft invented all this stuff. Microsoft doesn't go around telling people that; PC users just assume it.

I get into arguments all the time with PC users who will fight to the death on the idea that Microsoft invented the mouse. Microsoft never said that (as far as I know), but PC users believe that they are "the center of the universe," and if something good has been invented, it was invented for them (not copied from Apple).

I've even had PC users (on more than one occasion) try to tell me that Windows came out first, and that Apple is ripping off Microsoft. I think this is the core of why many Mac users hate Microsoft at the level that they do.

I think what really sizzles their bacon (I'm just one breakfast metaphor short of heading for the nearest Denny's), is that the product they consider to be "a cheap knockoff" of the Mac OS is the product that rules the computing world. How could a lesser product rise to the stature and dominance that it now maintains? How could the vast majority of the PC world not see what happened? Not see the difference? Not demand something better, especially when it's out there on the Macintosh platform? This is at the core of what still really toasts Mac users to this day.

Okay, now back to the question: Do I hate Microsoft? I think I used to, but now...honestly? I don't hate Microsoft. I certainly don't like Microsoft. I don't want to have a beer with Microsoft. I wouldn't let Microsoft date my sister, etc. But I don't hate them.

Like many Mac users, I'm just mad at Microsoft. It's not a love/ hate relationship because I don't love anything about Microsoft. It's more like a pissed/angry relationship. Why? It kind of goes back to that "Hey, you stole our idea" theory, but it's more than that. Mac users are mad because they're frustrated to be using a product (the Mac OS) that they know in their hearts is better. Not just a little better, a lot better. They know it's because most of them have at one time or another used PCs. They gave up the "unlimited software, cheap hardware, 50-joystick world" of the PC platform because they found something better. They want to share their discovery with the PC world they left behind. But the rest of the PC world not only doesn't know what they're missing, they flat out don't want to believe it.

I think it's because some big scary company has brainwashed them into believing they're using the best operating system there is. As long as they don't try another OS for themselves, they'll continue to believe it. What happens to PC users who do try the "other operating system" (the Mac)? Many of them never go back.

Here's how many Mac users feel. They use a computer that, hardware- and software-wise, is arguably the finest overall comput-ing platform there's ever been. It's certainly the most-imitated platform and that says something right there. It's also the most expensive, but the two generally go hand in hand. If you want the really good stuff, you have to pay for it. Mac users strongly feel they're using the absolute best computer. If it was a car, it would be a Lexus (Mercedes, BMW, etc.) while the rest of the computing world would be using a Ford Escort (nothing against the Ford Escort. It's dandy. It's just not a Lexus).

Now, want to get some insight into a Mac user's frustration? Picture yourself in your new Lexus, sitting at a stop light. A guy pulls up next to you in a Ford Escort. He rolls down the window, shakes his head, and starts laughing at you (by the way, for the sake of this metaphor, you know he's the PC user, right? That's you, the Mac user in the Lexus—just like in real life). You roll down your window and he says, "Man, I can't believe you bought a Lexus. What a bonehead! My car cost *way* less than yours, but it does all the same stuff: You've got air conditioning, I've got air conditioning. You've got cruise control, I've got cruise control. You've got power door locks, I've got power door locks, and I'm getting to where I want to go, just like you are, but for much less. I just don't get you Lexus guys," and he drives off. You sit there steaming at his ignorance.

He's right: You both do have an air conditioner, cruise control, and power door locks; but the experience of owning a fine motorcar like a Lexus is vastly different than the experience of owning an Escort (I don't own a Lexus myself, but I did drive an Escort long enough to know the difference).

Yes, the Lexus is more expensive. There's a reason—it's a world-class car. But try to explain that to the guy in the Escort. He just won't get it. To him, a car is a tool. A machine he uses to get him from point A to point B. That's all.

To you, your Lexus (like your Mac) is a work of art. A finely crafted automobile that you love to drive. You can hear that craftsmanship when you close the door. It sounds solid. It sounds tight. It sounds as if it was built by people who care how the door sounds when the owner shuts it. You go out of your way to drive your Lexus because it's fun, exciting, and it has personality.

The Lexus has an inherent value that is virtually impossible to explain to someone who hasn't owned a Lexus—you just have to own one to understand. It's the same with a Macintosh. The Mac has an inherent value, a personality, an excitement, that is virtually impossible to explain to a PC user who has never owned one. That's why you've probably never heard anyone use the phrase "PC fanatic." They're PC *users*. To them a PC is a *tool*. An appliance that gets them from point A to point B.

This is why Mac users are cranked at the PC industry as a whole. They feel PCs are the "Escort" of computers. Sure, they outsell the Mac, just like the Escort vastly outsells any Lexus (heck, the Escort alone probably outsells all Lexus models combined), but selling more product doesn't necessarily make it better. PC users act as if they believe that the only measure of a product's quality is how many people use it. If that were really the case, Ford could raise the price of their Escort by another $30,000, and *NSYNC would be the greatest band in the history of music because after all, right now they're selling the most records.

Arrogance or frustration?

You can probably see why Mac users might be upset with Microsoft, and you can understand why some PC users might be upset with Microsoft. But what PC users can't understand is why *Mac* users would be upset with Microsoft.

I'll give you a real-life example that happened to me not long ago, which shows how little PC users understand about us.

Some friends of mine own a local video-production studio, and we've been using their services for years. They're a small studio, but they do first-rate work and they've really built a name for themselves in our area. Up to this point, they've been doing most of their work traditionally (using video tape decks and analog technology) rather than doing everything on the computer and working digitally.

A couple of years ago, they realized that the video production industry was going all-digital and, although somewhat hesitant to abandon the technology that had gotten them this far, they were now seriously looking at computer-based, video-editing systems. They already had a PC in the studio (they had been running Photoshop on it for importing client logos and creating titles), and they had a couple of PCs they used for their accounting, business programs, etc. so they were (sadly) PC users (yet I still call them my "friends." Shocking, I know).

Because this was a big (and expensive) decision for them, every time I visited their studio, they would pick my brain about the Mac. Well, this once, it must have been getting close to decision time because they were really grilling me about the Mac and basically challenging me on why they should choose a Mac over a PC. After just a few minutes, I could tell that they didn't really want to be convinced. In fact, I could tell they had already decided to go with a PC-based Matrox system. I think what they were really looking for was any little snag or loophole in my argument so they would feel better about going against the industry standard and choosing a PC-based system.

As we went back and forth on the Mac versus PC thing, it was clear that they had all the same Mac misconceptions as anyone else who hadn't used a Mac, and much of their Macintosh information was provided by (you guessed it) PC users. I was dispelling their Mac misconceptions fairly easily, but at one point in the interrogation, one of the owners (we'll call him Tom—because that's his real name) made the comment, "But Macintosh users are so arrogant."

"Arrogant!" I replied. I then proceeded to make fun of his income bracket, the quality of this clothing, I questioned his upbringing, and generally let him know that I felt he was beneath me. (Is that what he meant by arrogant?)

Actually, what I told him was that most Mac users (at least the ones I've met) are among the nicest, most patient, fun-loving people you'd ever want to know. In some cases, they can also be quite defensive (for all the reasons I've mentioned in this book thus far). But what he was mistaking for arrogance is simply frustration. To help him understand the type of frustration a Mac user feels in a PC-oriented world, I gave him an analogy he could really relate to.

I said, "Tom, you guys are in the video production business. You've got a great shop, you were one of the first in our area, and you've built a solid reputation. By doing this, you've also created an extremely loyal client base." Then I described this scenario:

But let's say that tomorrow, a huge new video production company called "Video Production MegaWorld" (a totally made-up name) opens right down the street from your studio. Their studio is 10 times the size of your studio, and they have a huge staff and a huge marketing budget. For their grand opening, they take full-page ads in the local newspaper, and every time you turn on the TV, it seems that there is yet another ad for the grand opening of Video Production MegaWorld.

Pretty soon, everybody is talking about Video Production MegaWorld, so you finally go down there to see what all the fuss is about. As you walk in the door, you notice the bank of high-tech, flat-panel monitors that are running their "demo reel" (samples of their work designed to show potential clients the kind of work that they do). After watching for about two minutes, you realize that their demo reel looks an awful lot like the demo reel you guys have been sending out for the past year to your potential clients. In fact, you notice they've used a lot of the same camera angles and same effects, but overall you can tell these guys aren't nearly as good, because even though they were clearly "inspired" by your demo, in reality, their "knockoff" wasn't nearly as good.

You could sit there and point out where they didn't do particular things nearly as well as you had, where mistakes had clearly been made, and overall how their demo reel just isn't as good or as professional as your demo reel. You leave Video Production MegaWorld satisfied that if the public were to see their demo reel and yours, they'd clearly see the difference, and choose your firm over their marketing hype and fluff. So you head back to your office, confident that quality will win.

Back at your office, there's a call from one of your clients canceling a video project you were scheduled to shoot next week. The next day, you get another mysterious cancellation and then yet another.

Finally, when you get another cancellation, you put your customer on the spot and ask why they're canceling, and she reluctantly tells you she's having Video Production MegaWorld produce her spots. She tells you that a friend of hers went there and was pretty happy, and since they're offering "pretty much the same stuff that you guys do," she's now going there too. That's when you realize that she, and probably many of your other clients, simply can't tell the difference between your high-quality production work and Video Production MegaWorld's mediocre production work. Soon you're losing clients left and right to a company that produces lesser quality work but spends a bundle on marketing. It's a snowball effect—your clients are bombarded with Video Production MegaWorld ads on TV and in print, and now even some of your most loyal clients are using them—not because they're better, not because they offer something you don't, but primarily because "that's who everyone else is using."

Reality sets in

I asked him how he'd feel if he heard that people were now saying that Video Production MegaWorld is better than his studio. Or how would he react if he heard people saying that they think Tom actually copied his demo reel from the one running at Video Production MegaWorld?

Before long, Tom and his video company would become a niche player in the video production market. Why? Because Video Production MegaWorld spent a lot of money on marketing to convince the public to use a lesser product. The product of a company that was certainly not an innovator, but simply an imitator.

I told Tom that he now had an inside look at what it's like being a Macintosh user, and he readily admitted that he didn't realize what we were going through, and even went as far as to admit that he might have been wrong in his judgment about Macintosh. Oh, just in case you were wondering, of course they bought the PC system. In fact they bought two. I can provide all the ammo in the world, but it's very hard to overcome the fact that governs virtually all PC sales—everybody they know in the business uses PCs too.

We live in a world where people swear by a much lesser product. But we're not the only ones saying it. Even the leading

PC magazines constantly complain about numerous Windows bugs, tech support nightmares, never-ending virus worries, and shoddy workmanshipin many PC products. But their readers don't dare switch to Macintosh, because then they'd have to give up their choice of 50 joysticks, and they would have to use a product their neighbors don't use. That's very risky business indeed.

As a Macintosh user, you constantly wonder how the public can fail to see such an obvious difference. How can they be so blind? So brainwashed? So closeminded as to refuse to hear 30 million people who are screaming at the top of their lungs, "There's something better out there! It doesn't have to be like that!"? But then again, every time they turn on their TV, there's another ad for Microsoft, or Gateway or Intel.

The dangers of using PC logic

I've got to imagine part of the reason why PC users don't see the difference, or advantage, of Macintosh is how they make their decisions. Apparently, years ago they were told "don't buy a Macintosh" and they were given a list of reasons that may or may not have been legitimate at that time (which could have been eight or ten years ago). Even if they heard it all 10 years ago, that's the way it still must be, right? They've never thought of re-evaluating that initial Mac info, and in ten years, really…how much could things have changed in the computing world?

It's almost as if PC users make a judgment on which computer platform to use, not by which one is actually better but which one offers the widest selection of keyboards and joysticks.

I wonder what my own life would be like if I made my important buying decisions the same way PC users do. In fact, let's do that. Let's apply PC logic to a hypothetical purchase—buying a new car. (By now you've learned that all my analogies are about cars, and all my metaphors are about breakfast. Now, if I could stop writing long enough to get in my car to drive to breakfast, I'd be set.)

Buying a car is a serious decision, so I thought I'd ask my friends and co-workers which car I should buy. I talked with lots of different car owners, including my neighbor who is a self-proclaimed car expert. After carefully weighing their input, I've narrowed my car search down to two cars: a Mercedes-Benz C320 Sedan (an entry-level Mercedes) that's a bit more expensive than the Buick Regal Limited Edition that I'm also considering. (I'm giving Ford a break this time. Again, there's nothing wrong with a Buick Regal, I just need another popular car for this analogy.) Now, it's time to use PC logic to find out which car is really the better choice. Here goes…

Accessories

First stop—the big auto parts store in town. I have to admit this was a big eye-opener, because they had considerably more parts for Buicks than they did for Mercedes. In fact, it seemed as if they had fully ten times more Buick parts. Take floormats, for example. They had dozens of floormats for Buicks, in every style and color. However, they had only four that would fit a Mercedes. Also, there were just a few colors available in Mercedes floormats, but there were all kinds of colors available for the Buick—red, blue, brown, gray—you name it.

Later that day I went to the automotive department at Kmart. I asked the salesperson in the department where "the Mercedes accessories section" was, and she just started laughing. She sarcastically told me it was next to the brandy snifters and candelabras. But when I asked her to show me where the Buick department was, she told me that Buick parts were all over the entire automotive department—from spark plugs to mufflers, floormats to radios. In fact, there was so much available for the Buick Regal, it made me realize just how popular the Buick Regal must be. This Regal must be some car!

Repairs

Maintenance is an issue of major concern to me, so I did a little research. It seems that the Mercedes did have advantages in this area, but I have to tell you, I could find a Buick Regal repair manual just about anywhere they sell Buick parts (which is just about everywhere). Apparently Buick Regal owners love to tinker with their Regals, because at the book store there were dozens of books on how to repair your Regal and how to customize your Regal, but quite frankly, there wasn't much on repairing your Mercedes. Hmmm. This had me concerned.

More is better!

I did a little research online, and according to figures supplied by the U.S. Department of Commerce (in November of 2001), Mercedes represented only a 1.4% share of the U.S. auto market. 1.4%!!!! That scares me. What if Mercedes were to go out of business? Then what? How would I get parts, and what if people stopped making accessories? Sure, I know Mercedes is a big company and is making profits now, and selling lots of cars, and they've been around for years, but this is frightening stuff. Even though I only plan on keeping this car a couple of years, what if the unthinkable happens and Mercedes goes under? This decision is becoming more obvious every minute.

Buying the car

Another thing that surprised me was that about the only place I could find a new Mercedes is at a Mercedes dealer, and there are only three of them in the entire tri-country area where I live. But Buicks you can find at a dozen or more dealers, and you can find a used Buick on every used-car lot in town; but finding a used Mercedes is like finding a needle in a haystack. It's so obvious that many more people buy Buicks than buy Mercedes. This is all becoming so clear.

The need for speed

Apparently, Mercedes has been running ads showing how much faster Mercedes are than Buicks. In fact, in certain real-world tests the Mercedes was nearly twice as fast as the Buick. Although Mercedes does cite the sources for their testing and details on how the tests were performed, it can't really be true, can it? I mean, I had always heard that Mercedes were slow, and all my friends who have Buicks tell me how fast they are, and they say their Buicks are faster than a Mercedes (even though they admit, they've never tried to test them side by side). I mean seriously, could things have changed that much in the past few years that Mercedes are now faster than Buicks? Mercedes must be lying. It just can't be.

The bottom line

Admittedly, there are a number of things I like about the Mercedes. It comes with more standard features than the Buick, and it definitely wins in the looks department. Also, apparently Mercedes require less maintenance, less troubleshooting, are easier to use, and according to Mercedes' claims, they're faster. I was also particularly intrigued with how many Mercedes owners absolutely love their cars, and swear they wouldn't have anything but a Mercedes (they're almost fanatical about them—buying Mercedes again and again, year after year).

However, the fact of the matter is there are clearly not as many accessories for the Mercedes, not nearly as many places to buy a Mercedes, they're more expensive, and their market share is so small I'm concerned that one day they might go out of business. Besides, all my friends have Buicks, and they even use Buicks at work. I think it's a pretty safe bet to go with the Buick, so that's what I bought. Now that I have my Buick, I have to say that it does a perfectly good job of getting me from point A to point B, and after buying it, I immediately bought a new set of floormats, right at the local auto parts store. My new Buick is very functional. I'm not "in love with it" like those Mercedes fanatics are, but I'm not supposed to be. It's a car, right? It's designed to get me where I'm going. Right?

Through their eyes

If you were to use PC logic, you'd buy the Buick. You'd buy it because: It has more accessories, all your friends have one, your co-workers have one, it's cheaper, and because to you it's just a tool. If we all made important decisions like PC users made their platform decision, this would be a totally beige world. So why do so many PC users think this way? Is it a chemical imbalance in their brain? I don't think so (though some Mac users would definitely argue this point). I think it's because "that's what they have been told." Who told them this? Two sources: the PC-biased media and Microsoft. It's Microsoft's job to tell the public how great their software is, so I don't really blame them—that's business. But the media is another story.

Making the news

In my opinion, the biggest problem Apple has ever had is how they are abused, attacked, berated, and outright lied about in the mainstream and computing world media. It's the reason why I got into the Macintosh publishing business in the first place—to tell the other side of the story.

I honestly couldn't take reading press reports, TV news reports, and magazine articles that were so patently misleading, so "anti-Apple," so twisted to show only one side of the story. So Jim Workman and I founded *Mac Today* back in 1993 as our way of combating the lies, and creating an outlet for the other side of the story. A story about the great things Apple was doing, about their triumphs, heroes, and the good news about Apple that the mainstream press absolutely was purposely ignoring.

In Chapter 1, I gave you my reasons why I thought the press was so anti-Apple: In short, the mainstream media are PC people. They use PCs, they accept PCs, they write their anti-Apple articles on PCs. They see Apple as "outside the mainstream" (which it is), therefore they want to see it fail. If they can help it fail, then they've done their job. Before the iMac was introduced, only one kind of news about Apple was being reported—bad news. If something bad happened, it was on the cover of magazines the next week. If Packard Bell was in trouble, it was buried on page 36. If Apple was in trouble, it was on the front cover. Magazines like *Wired* would run a harsh story about Apple, complete with an Apple logo on the cover, surrounded by barbed wire, and simply the word "Pray." What do you think that kind of imagery does for Apple's sales? Does that make you feel that buying an Apple computer is "a safe bet?"

I would spend barrels of ink in *Mac Today,* issue after issue, picking apart these news reports and articles that were so one-sided, so unfair, and so obviously "out to get Apple" that I'm amazed that Apple was able to weather the storm.

Yet Apple outlasted leading PC companies (of whom the press were totally enamored) like Packard Bell, NEC, and Digital. At this writing, it appears that PC giant Compaq will be gobbled up by Hewlett-Packard. Apple has outlasted them all, with a relatively small marketshare. How have they pulled off this mini-miracle? Apple is different. It's not like other PC companies, and that's what the PC industry analysts and Wall Street analysts can't figure out.

They just don't "get it." They don't get Apple. They try to apply the same logic to Apple that they do to Packard Bell. But they don't understand that Apple has a strategic advantage that Packard Bell never had—people *care* about Apple. Apple doesn't have customers; it has a fan club. It has a dedicated, fanatical, Apple-or-nothing customer base. It has the kind of customer base every PC company would dream of having but none does.

That's why so many analysts use the same old tired "Apple may go the same way as Amiga" or "Apple may go the same way as Beta video tapes. Beta was better, but more people used VHS, so VHS won the war." They just don't "get" Apple. Never have.

Part of the problem of not "getting" Apple is the fact that the crutch the media and analysts use to measure whether Apple will make it or not is market share. To them, it's all about market share. Which is weird, because what keeps people in business is profits, not market share. Want proof? Where's Packard Bell? At one time they were the leading PC manufacturer in the world. They had more market share than anyone. But they're long gone. Market share didn't save them, and Apple outlasted them.

Wait! How can that be? Apple, with only about 4% of the market, outlasting the PC company that had the largest market share in the world? That's right. Because Apple was able to do something that Packard Bell wasn't able to do—continue to make profits. Apple is profitable even today when the tech industry is going through what is perhaps the biggest slump in the industry's history. Huge PC companies are posting record losses, quarter after quarter, with massive layoffs. Apple, on the other hand, has just posted back-to-back quarterly profits, and has billions of dollars in the bank, in cash. Where are the cover stories "Apple bucks the downtown" or "Apple profits while PC companies go bust"? Where is the *Wired* cover that shows a halo above the Apple logo and says, "We were wrong!"?

To this day, you'll find reports every week predicting Apple's doom. It's just what the mainstream media is programmed to do.

I remember just over five years ago reading an article by Jake Kirchner in the April 1996 issue of *PC Magazine.* In it he said, "No doubt a bitter group of Macintosh users will feel the sting of Apple's demise. I'm sure there will be a large, forlorn group of Apple users who will struggle along supported only by one another, their online postings becoming increasingly bitter as we close out the millenium." Macintosh users haven't felt that sting yet, because almost six years later, Apple's still here.

Or how about that same year when *Rolling Stone* ran a two-part cover story on "The Death of Apple." Because it was on the cover, you didn't even have to read the article to get the message.

How wrong has the media been? Look at it this way. They started predicting that Apple would go out of business about 30 seconds after Apple introduced the Mac back in 1984. They've been predicting it ever since, and every single prediction, every single time someone said, "Apple's not out of the woods yet," every single time some highly paid analysts said, "Apple's not going to make it," they were absolutely wrong.

Despite all of this, despite Apple's outlasting companies 10 times their size, despite producing profits when their PC competitors are in the midst of massive layoffs, the best and brightest analysts in the industry still cling to their misguided market share theory. It's not really a theory. It's a myth. Why don't you read reports that say, "With its small market share, BMW isn't going to be able to compete," or, "With significantly less than 1% of the U.S. market, how can Volvo go up against the big three"? It's because in that industry, they understand that market share isn't what it's all about. In the auto industry, the media isn't all lined up against Subaru, BMW, Volvo, Mercedes, Jaguar, and Lexus (which ALL have less market share in the automotive market than Apple has in the computing market). They know that it's profits that count, not market share, or none of those auto makers would still be in business today.

You can't look at Apple the way you look at other PC companies, because no other PC company is like Apple. No other PC company makes both the operating system and the computer that runs it. Not Compaq. Not Gateway. Not even Microsoft.

I think the biggest market share mistake these analysts make is unfairly pitting Apple's market share against the entire PC industry as a whole, stacking up the *combined* market share of every PC company against just Apple (rather than comparing Apple's market share to Micron's or Gateway's). That's at the heart of the problem. Apple doesn't have to beat the entire PC industry to stay in business. They don't have to beat the entire PC industry to make a profit, and they don't have to grow their market to make a profit, because Apple's market share has definitely contracted in the past few years, but they're still making profits. This just doesn't make sense to PC industry analysts, so Apple pays the price for analyst ignorance.

The wisdom of analysts

When the tech slump really hit, Apple warned Wall Street that their earnings would be lower than expected. Apple stock dropped about 50% the next day. They didn't announce layoffs, bankruptcy, or massive losses, just lower earnings, in an industry where everybody was announcing lower earnings. Rather than looking at the situation rationally and judging Apple as another company feeling the same effects as the rest of the industry, the market jumped on Apple with two feet, and sent its stock tumbling.

My stockbroker called to let me know what had happened (he knows I'm interested in Apple, but I didn't have any Apple stock at that time). I asked him what his firm's analysts were saying. He said they thought that Apple's market share wasn't growing, and that sales of Macintosh computers were mostly to existing Macintosh users, and they weren't making inroads in the PC market.

What a shocker! That's the same exact thing analysts were saying a week before the drop. A year before the drop. Five years before the drop. In fact, that's what analysts who don't understand Apple have always said. I took this as a clear signal to buy, and I bought some Apple stock (which I still hold). I thought that if the analysts had come up with something new, some new revelation that I hadn't heard about Apple before, then I might sit on the sidelines. But if they were touting the same old "market share crap," then I knew that their opinion (which has always been wrong) would be wrong once again (after all, they have a perfect track record).

I figured it this way: The day before the 50% drop in Apple's share price, most of the major Wall Street firms had a "buy" recommendation on Apple stock. The day before the drop they were completely wrong about Apple. Now, overnight, after being wrong, they're suddenly right? What about their customers who bought Apple stock the day, week, or month before the drop based on their "buy" recommendations? You don't hear the analysts lining up to apologize for that or admitting they were wrong. Again.

It's like I always say: When it comes to analysts, the first four letters say it all.

But where are the developers!

Another thing industry analysts love to glom onto is the myth that fewer and fewer companies are developing software for the Mac, which is total bull; today there's probably more software for the Macintosh than at any time in history.

Believe it or not, there are probably even more Mac *games* now than any time in history. But here's the catch—remember how I mentioned in the chapter about CompUSA, about all those hybrid software packages, and how both the PC and Mac versions were on the same disc, but they were sold in the PC department? Well, in the industry's calculations of how much Mac software is sold, when a hybrid CD is sold in the PC section to a Mac user, do you think CompUSA counts that as a sale of PC software or Mac software? Since they don't ask which platform you're using when you buy this hybrid software, which platform gets credited with the sale? Hmmmm. Makes you stop and think, doesn't it?

Now, don't get me wrong, I'm not trying in any way to say that there's as much Mac software as PC software. There just isn't, plain and simple, and this has long been a thorn in the side of Mac fanatics.

Years ago, back in the dark days of Macintosh, when software selection was pretty thin, we used to e-mail PC software companies to try to convince them they'd have a robust new market if they'd port their software over to the Mac. Guy Kawasaki's daily "EvangeList" e-mail newsletter was a great help back then in rallying Mac users to send polite e-mail letters to software vendors to let them know they have an untapped market ready and willing to buy their products. I used to read his newsletter faithfully, and I was one of those crazed Mac fanatics who wrote to those companies. Every time I'd run across a PC software developer who had a great program that wasn't being developed for the Mac, I'd send a letter trying to convince them of the error of their ways—serving just one side of the market.It used to really keep me up at night, but now luckily when it comes to Mac software, things are decidedly better. Plus, I now totally understand that I was the one in the wrong in the first place.

You see, I realized that I was looking at the whole issue from one side. A Mac user's side. I was angry that PC users were getting some cool software that I couldn't get, so I started whining. But when I finally took a step back, took a deep breath, and looked at things from a PC developer's point of view, I then realized that developing for the PC has a ton of advantages that just aren't available when developing for the Macintosh platform.

I'm not just talking sheer numbers here, I'm talking about people. PC people. As customers, PC people offer some distinct advantages that actually make them a far more desirable target market than Mac users. For example:

(1) PC users are very patient

A patient customer is an ideal customer, and PC users are famous for their patience. For example, apparently they don't mind sitting on hold for hours waiting for tech support. They're used to it, it's a part of their lives, and they don't seem to mind it one bit. As a developer, this amounts to a huge savings because you don't have to waste money hiring a huge tech support staff—just put a few temps in a room, with a couple of incoming phone lines, and give them the same printed instruction manual that comes with the software to begin with (which you can be sure the caller has never read), and you're in business.

(2) PC users are thrifty shoppers

Since the main determining factor in any PC user's decision is low price (not quality, ease of use, dependability, or meaningless things like those), you don't have to waste time and money creating a quality product—you only have to be concerned with making a cheap one. The cheaper, the better. You can cut all kinds of corners, ship software rife with bugs and obvious flaws, and save loads of cash by skipping the whole pre-release testing phase altogether. You don't have to concern yourself with trivial matters like compatibility or ease of installation. Just make sure it's dirt cheap, and you're guaranteed to sell your product by the truckload.

(3) PC users are great listeners

You have to admire the way PC users listen to software and hardware companies. You tell them something, anything, and they'll believe it. For example, I remember seeing TV ads for a PC chip maker touting that their new chip was going to completely change the PC user's Internet experience. I remember thinking to myself, "Hey, it's not a cable modem or a high-tech piece of Web-enhancing software. It's just a computer chip that goes slightly faster than their old chip." But that didn't stop millions of PC users from marching right out to upgrade their old machines for new ones that would "enhance their Internet experience." That's an ideal customer—you tell them what you want them to do, and even if it doesn't make sense, they'll do it anyway. You've gotta love that.

(4) PC users are incredibly forgiving

If you're a PC software company, you can sell PC users products that have lots of bugs and compatibility problems. You can have them jump through hoops installing the programs, and you can really stick it to them by now making existing programs on their hard drives incompatible with the new software they just installed. You can create software that has them spending more time troubleshooting their computer than actually being productive with it, and they'll still line up at midnight outside the computer superstore to be the first to have the honor to pay for the privilege. That, my friends, is one forgiving customer, and the type of consumer you want as a registered user of your products.

PC users are much more forgiving than, say, automobile customers, because if they buy a product and it breaks down numerous times, those whining bellyaching car buyers call for a "Lemon Law" to be enacted, so they can take their car back to the dealer and get a full refund. Not so with PC users. If the software crashes their computer over and over, and generally makes their life a living hell for days on end, what do they do? Reinstall the old software they bought from you last year, or wait patiently for a bug fix (that may never come). God bless these incredibly forgiving people.

(5) PC users are diligent

These are not lazy people, no sir. They think nothing of staying up all night trying to track down a virus, or hunting down which incompatible driver is causing their system to crash over and over again. They're very diligent—nothing stops them. Crashes, viruses, bugs, conflicts, peripherals that don't work—they don't give up; they keep going and going and going. These are the types of people who make great customers. They're willing to do their share of the work so you, the developer, don't have to.

(6) PC users aren't easily swayed

You don't have to worry too much about losing your customers to a superior computing platform; you've got these guys hooked! Even though many industry experts will readily admit that there is a significantly more stable, more reliable, easier-to-use operating system out there, you don't have to worry about them "jumping ship" and switching to something better. It's as if they're blinded. Brainwashed if you will; and you're the lucky beneficiary of their shortsightedness. Don't worry about someone changing their mind; it's already made up—they're PC users for life—have your way with them.

(7) PC users are waiting for your lead

PC users live by a golden rule: If their friends and co-workers use it, then it must be right. When it comes time to make a serious purchase, some people start researching the products, comparing models, looking at specs, analyzing their personal needs, etc. Not PC people. They look directly to their peers to find out which system *they're* using, then buy a similar system. They will often even seek the advice of people who know less about computers than they themselves do, but they do it anyway to ensure that their decision is supported by the masses—that they are following the pack.

Seriously, think about it—how many times have you heard one of your neighbors ask another neighbor which PC they should buy? It's scary. The reason they do is that because they have so many problems with their current PC, they don't trust their own judgment. By looking at their previous choices, I don't blame them one bit.

As a developer for the PC platform, their indecisiveness is your gain. Don't worry about spending millions to "get the customer." Get to their neighbors, their co-workers, and you've got a customer who will "follow your lead" for life.

(8) PC users have short memories

If you have a product that isn't selling well, give it a new name that sounds similar to a product that actually is selling well, and PC users will probably forget which is which, and maybe buy yours.

For example, Apple's iMac broke about every computing sales record in the book. It revolutionized the industry. So, if you have a line of PCs that isn't breaking records, create a product that has a similar sounding name. For example, a short time after the iMac came out, Compaq created a computer called the "iPac." Only one letter is different. Not bad! Or how about the "eOne" from eMachines? Same number of letters—also not a bad try. By employing a similar strategy, there's a decent chance that a hapless PC user might mistake your "sound-alike" for the hot-selling brand, and buy yours by accident. Boom—you've got a sale! Luckily, PC users don't remember trivial details like "exact names" and colors. Luckily for you, the only thing PC users have been programmed to remember is megahertz. They know they need a lot of them (to enhance their Internet experience, no doubt). Face it, PC users never would've upgraded to Windows 98 if they had any recollection of the night-

mare they encountered when upgrading to Windows 95. Their lack
of memory can be a windfall to your sales.

(9) PC users don't need variety

Thinking of creating a bold new product in a wide variety of colors?
Don't waste your money. PC users apparently love beige. It's the
color of their lives. Everything they use is beige: their computer,
mouse, keyboard, monitor, you name it. Learn from the PC manufacturers that tried to follow the success of Apple's iMac by coming
out with computers that featured large chunks of translucent plastic
in a variety of colors. Not one had a hit on their hands. Why?
Because PC users don't need variety.

The PC personality craves order, uniformity, a controlled environment that stifles creativity and self-expression. They like to be
told what do, what to buy, and they like it in one color—beige. As
a developer, you can save development costs, time, and money by
simply creating your product in beige and no one will complain.
Remember, things that are repeated become pleasant.

(10) PC users have a sense of humor

Sure, they may seem humorless on the surface, but you can pull
a trick or two on them, and they'll just shake their heads and laugh.
For example, when a reporter for one of the big PC magazines got
hold of an internal Microsoft document revealing that Microsoft was
aware that Windows 2000 had more than 63,000 known bugs but
went ahead and shipped it anyway, the PC community just laughed,
shook their heads, then got in line to buy their copies. Nothing
rattles these PC users; they just laugh it off and hand over their
checks.

They obviously know how to take a joke, and apparently some PC developers know how to tell one. If you're looking for a customer whom you can easily tell, "the joke's on you!" then the PC market is an audience that needs no warming up.

It's all about just one thing

As you can see, if you're a software/hardware developer, the choice between developing for the Macintosh market (which requires spending a bundle on silly things like quality control, testing, industrial design, support, and [dare I mention] color) and the PC market (where quality, customer service, color, ease of use, support, and other trivial matters are not your concern) is pretty clear. It's a simple choice: Developing for the PC platform costs less, which means developers can make more money—and isn't that what it's all about? The money. Maybe that's why many PC developers never develop a Mac-compatible product, and stay right where they are—where the money is. And where millions of those funny, patient, loyal, forgiving, diligent customers stand ready for you to give them their next buying instruction. Gees, it all makes sense now.

The battle lines are drawn

If you haven't yet made the jump to Mac fanatic, be assured of this:

(1) You will (make the jump, that is).
(2) You will hate at least part of Microsoft (the part that makes Windows), if not all of it.
(3) You will wind up using at least some Microsoft software and you'll feel guilty about it, but use it anyway.

(4) You will wind up absolutely pulling your hair out over the incredible bias in the mainstream media against Apple (and you'll realize why so many Mac users become prematurely bald).

(5) All this will make you even more attached to your Mac, and make you want to show even more people "the light." It's weird, but that's the way it works.

CHAPTER TEN

The 20 most important things I've learned about being a Mac user

Back when I first got into the Mac, I had to learn every thing the hard way. I'm not talking about the simple things like "Don't forget to rebuild your desktop once a week" or "Disable your extensions at start-up by holding the Shift key." I'm talking about life. Mac life. Real life. The things you could only learn from veteran Mac users (people who used Macs in the war).

These cantankerous old veteran Mac users would gather around and scream at you, like military drill sergeants, while you did wide-grip push-ups down in the dirt. They would tell you how hard your Mac life was going to be. How alone you would feel. How "soft" you were. They'd ask you if you wanted "the naked truth." They'd ask you again and again, louder and louder, "Do you want the naked truth?" When you'd finally break, and answer, "Yes, yes! I want the truth!" they'd just yell back "You can't handle the truth!" (They stole all their lines from military movies.) But the more they screamed, the stronger it made you. It made you a Mac survivor. After going through that, you felt you could face the cold, dead stare of even the angriest, most frustrated, ugliest PC user and come out alive. You had crossed over.

Frankly, I don't want to see you go through what I had to. So I'm going to do for you what I wish someone had done for me back when I was still a Mac private. I'm going to share with you the 20 most important things, the most important truths I've learned about being a Mac user.

Some of this may seem shocking at first. Even brutal. You may not want to read this alone. Get a Mac buddy and I promise you—you'll get through this together. Let us begin:

(1) Macs are more expensive than PCs

However, when you compare, feature for feature, the real value between a similarly configured Mac and a brand name PC, you'll find that...well...the PC is still cheaper. (Rats, where was I going with this one?) It's true. In the current market, a similarly configured PC is cheaper, but like almost every product, you get what you pay for. A similarly configured PC does not equal a Macintosh computer. That's why Macs are slightly more expensive.

You've probably seen ads where you can buy a computer package that includes a leading brand of PC, packed with MHz, RAM, and hard-drive space, bundled with a 15" flat-panel monitor, keyboard, mouse, two stereo speakers, and a color inkjet printer, all for just $999 (at least, I've seen that ad).

Now, you're probably thinking "Hey, a decent iMac costs about that much, and that's just the iMac—no printer, no stereo speakers, no flat-panel monitor—just the iMac. What gives?" What gives is that a PC isn't an iMac. If you want something better than a beige box of crap, you'll have to pay a little bit more.

(2) Steve is the right person to lead Apple

From stories I've read, and from firsthand accounts, Steve Jobs is unlikely to win any "nice guy" awards from his fellow employees at Apple. Over the years I've read many stories about his temper, his ego, his tirades, and firing of employees who just happen to be in the wrong place at the wrong time. Those stories may or may not be true, but there's one thing I am absolutely certain of: Steve's the right man to lead Apple. There's never been anyone at Apple who has had the impact that Steve has had since his return. He may be a tyrant, demanding, unforgiving, and the worst boss ever. But he's also a visionary. A genius. A man that gets things done. And the man that kept Apple afloat when a host of other "nice guys" couldn't.

(3) Stay out of the computer sections of office supply stores or big consumer electronics stores

In fact, stay out of all PC stores, don't read PC catalogs, and just steer clear of any place that looks as if it might carry PC hardware, software, or peripherals (with the exception of CompUSA for the reasons I listed earlier). I promise you, wandering through aisles and aisles of computer stuff that's not for you will not make you feel good. For example, many people enjoy simply looking around an exotic car showroom with no intention of buying. They ogle the Ferraris, Turbo Porches, and Lamborghinis, and think to themselves, "I'd love to have one of these babies." Looking through the PC department is different. You're not seeing things you can't afford, or things you dream of—you're seeing aisle after aisle of things that look as if they should be for you, but simply aren't. This isn't window shopping, it's personally destructive behavior. You'll leave the department feeling frustrated, angry, and perhaps confused. Do yourself a favor—just avoid those sections and I guarantee, you'll be happier for it.

(4) Want to feel really great about owning a Mac? Subscribe to some PC magazines

I could go on and on about what a nightmare Windows is and I could tell you about all the problems PC users face every day. But since I make no bones about the fact that I'm totally biased toward Apple, it just doesn't have the same impact as it would if you read actual PC users slamming Microsoft, Windows, and the overall PC nightmare.

That's why in most issues of *Mac Today*, I would highlight articles that actually appeared in real PC magazines. They were fantastic because there's nothing more potent than reading where the editors of PC magazines slam Microsoft, detailing their own Windows nightmares, and going on and on about constant problems, conflicts, shoddy quality, bugs, and what life is really like on the PC platform.

When you hear them saying these things about their own platform, it does a better job of telling the story than I ever could. It's magic!

A couple of quick examples:

In the March 2000 issue of the PC gaming magazine, *Computer Games*, Denny Atkins drags Microsoft over the coals in his "Up Front" column "Shattered Windows." He chronicles how he "…lost yet another evening of my life to reinstalling Windows," and he calls Microsoft Windows, "The most challenging game."

He goes on to say, "It's the rare gamer who hasn't cursed Windows at some point," and adds that Bill Gates is not to blame, because "It took a huge team to create such a sophisticated, catastrophic program." (Did you catch that? A PC guy "in the know" calling Windows a "catastrophic program." You gotta love that!)

But that's nothing compared to the October 1998 issue of *PC World*. This was a Windows-bashing field day.

On page 64, there's an article entitled, "Bugged by Windows 98? Glitches are driving users up the wall." It includes an illustration of a PC on fire and its owner holding his head in disbelief. The article starts with the story of an office worker who installed Windows 98 and the software crashed during start-up. The damage was so severe that "it took her two days to recover her data." And the *PC World* article noted that "…nightmarish installation is far from an isolated incident.

Another article on page 51 titled, "You've got mail! (Boom!)" is about PC viruses that can attach themselves to e-mail and can (their words) "put you out of business." (See what you're missing?)

And yet another article on page 45 is called "Windows 98—without the bugs." Their solution to having Windows 98's troubleshooting features, but without all the Windows 98 bugs, is to not use Windows 98 at all, and instead "Beef up Windows 95 with utilities that offer the same—or better—tools."

On page 19 of that same issue, Phil Lemmons (then *PC World's* Editorial Director) writes an editorial, "My Two Tips for PC Troubleshooting," telling his own nightmares of upgrading PC hardware and software. He says "I installed Windows 98 only to have it die at the splash screen." After encountering problem after problem, he writes, "Days and sleepless nights later, I sheepishly asked the *PC World* Test Center for help." They eventually fixed Phil's problems. This is amazing! This guy is a PC *expert*, the Editorial Director for a leading PC magazine, and yet he has to resort to calling his magazine's Test Center to get help. What do normal people do, who don't have a "Test Center" to call for help with their nightmares?

PC World's December 1998 issue had a back page editorial by Stephen Maines called, "Can this machine be stopped?" His article details his problems with (get this) shutting down his PC (in both Windows 95 and 98). The pull quote from the article pretty much says it all: "Since when should shutting down and restarting a PC be almost as complex as running a nuclear power plant?" His entire article is a testament to how overly complex and trouble-prone Windows and PCs are.

PC Magazine also gets in on the PC bash fest. In their August 2000 issue there's an article by Bill Machrone called "Life is Too Short." The article chronicles the amazing set of problems he encountered trying to edit a home video he shot of a skit that his son and a classmate wrote and staged for a class project.

He tells how he struggles for days without success. He goes to CompUSA, buys different video capture cards, and even tries using different PCs, but he still can't edit his video on his PC.

Finally, in frustration, he contacts a fellow *PC Magazine* editor who lives nearby, and this guy lends him his new Sony laptop that comes bundled with video-editing software. As you might expect, they can't get that to work either. Finally, with the deadline looming, they give up and edit the video, not on a PC at all, but manually using two VCRs and dubbing from tape to tape.

The closing line of his article says it all: "Between us, we've got lots of computer experience. Without troubleshooting time, though, the technology left us high and dry. As my wife said, what do normal people do?"

Here's my point (and the point I think the author was trying to make as well): If two editors of the nation's largest computer magazine can't get video editing to work on a PC, what chance do regular PC users have? This is a real-life snapshot of what many PC users' lives are really like. Pretty scary stuff.

These are just little snippets of the amazing, hilarious, and stunning articles you'll find in nearly every issue of these PC magazines. If you really want to hear somebody give it to Microsoft, you'll find it there. That's why I always encourage *Mac Today* readers to subscribe to some of these PC magazines to learn that what they're really missing is misery, troubleshooting, frustration, and wasted days and night. I can't tell you how many letters I've received over the years from *Mac Today* readers thanking me for convincing them to subscribe to these PC magazines.

In fact, if Apple really wants to keep customers for life, they should include at least one PC magazine subscription with every iMac sold.

(5) Apple will make some bold moves that will freak your ass out

Apple is a company that innovates. That takes chances. That tries new ideas. That's why they've always led the industry. But leading the industry involves making some very bold moves—like being the first company to do away with floppy disks. It shocked the industry (and Mac users) and was criticized by almost everybody. That was, until the rest of the industry started to follow suit.

Apple was the first company to add built-in CD-ROM drives to computers. Now every computer has a CD-ROM drive of some sort. The thing is—Apple's not done. They're going to make some decisions to add, or do away with, some things that will totally freak you out. Don't let it. What you're seeing is the future developing before your eyes, and history being made at the same time. Just go with it because, whatever it is, before long everybody else will be doing it too.

(6) Make some Mac friends

Being a Macintosh user is like most everything else in life—it's better if you share it with someone. Having someone to share your triumphs and tribulations can really make the experience much richer. It also gives you a built-in support network when you have a really harsh encounter with a total PC Weenie. Plus, you'll uncover so many neat things about the Mac, about the OS, about a cool piece of shareware, or a new Mac gadget, that you'll be dying to tell somebody who cares. That's what "Mac buddies" are all about, and cultivating one or more of them is highly recommended.

(7) Go to a Macworld Expo keynote

I've been going to Macworld Expo since 1993, but I always skipped the keynote presentation from Apple. I just didn't want to drag my butt out of bed at 6:30 in the morning and stand in a line with thousands of other people just to hear Steve Jobs tell me what I can read on the Web, or watch with QuickTime streaming in the comfort of my hotel room. Finally, one year I went ahead, braved the line and watched the keynote live. If I tell you "it was well worth it," that would be the understatement of the year. Steve Jobs is a fantastic public speaker. No, actually, he's more than that—he's a fantastic motivational speaker, and his presentations (yes, I've braved the line many times since then) literally electrify the crowd. I was actually surprised at how I got swept up in the moment, and how I would leap to my feet cheering when he'd show some new Apple innovation. You really felt that you were part of something special. You were seeing the future unfold right there on stage, and the electricity in the air and the excitement in the room are really overwhelming. It's like an Apple rock concert and Steve's the star.

If you're really into the Mac, and want to experience "Macdom" at a whole new level, get up early, get in line, and I promise you it's something you'll always remember.

(8) Always wait for the OS updater

When Apple introduces a major overhaul of its OS, the first version is always, well, not all it could be. People who've been at this awhile, have learned to sit out the first release, and patiently wait just a little bit for Apple to release the inevitable free update.

For example, when Apple released Mac OS 8, the smart ones waited for Mac OS 8.1 before making the plunge. When Apple introduced Mac OS 8.5, the smart ones waited for Mac OS 8.6 to take a dip in that pool. Remember OS 9? Hopefully, you remember OS 9.1. How about the long-awaited Mac OS X? Mac veterans waited a bit longer, for Mac OS X version 10.1. Want your OS experience to be smoother? Want to keep most of the hair on your head? Remember, good things come to those who wait.

(9) Don't watch Microsoft ads on TV

When you see a Microsoft ad on TV, seriously, change the channel. There's nothing to be gained from watching a Microsoft ad—it can only bring trouble, because Microsoft often has some very compelling ads. When you see one of these it makes you mad. Not at Microsoft, at Apple. Because you wonder why Apple ads aren't as compelling. In fact, it seems like Microsoft ads do all the things that you wish Apple would do. It will make you start to think that for once Apple should start copying Microsoft. My advice? Skip the whole thing and change channels. You'll be glad you did.

(10) When you first meet new people, don't tell them you use Macintosh

You'll find that this is information that's better digested at the right time. It's kind of like being a virgin. It's a great thing, but you don't necessarily want to use it as an icebreaker at a party. You really only want to mention it when the timing is right.

Also, don't mention it if you're with a group of people standing anywhere near the edge of an active volcano (the virgin thing, not the Mac thing).

(11) Always buy the fastest Mac you can afford

I've had people ask me so many times over the years, "Should I get a 733-MHz or the 800-MHz model?" My advice? Always, always buy the fastest machine you can afford. I guarantee you'll never be sitting there in front of your Mac saying, "Gee, I wish I had bought the slower model." It just doesn't happen. Actually, I've heard a variation of that sentence, but it was spoken by a PC user who chose a PC over a Mac. He said, "I think I bought the slower machine."

(12) Some of the best things about the Mac OS don't come with your Mac

That's right—the Mac OS's ability to be customized to suit your own tastes, through shareware and free extensions and control panels, is part of the beauty of the Mac. You can expand the Mac's power, and really make it "your Mac," by adding all sorts of cool features to your

System. You just drop them in the System Folder and the System automatically puts them right where they belong. Restart your Mac, and you can have a whole new experience. A new look, new features, more power, or more fun. Check out www.macdownloads.com, and start customizing your Mac right away.

(13) Even though Macs aren't sold as business machines, they're great for doing business

Now don't get me wrong. I think Macs are great business machines, but you have to admit—Macs are, and have always been, designed from the ground up as machines for creative work. Why do you think Apple shows off the Mac's speed using Adobe Photoshop? It's what Macs do best—run graphics!

Macs have always ruled the graphics market and they still do today. Over the years, Apple has tried numerous times to crack into that lucrative business market, but to this day the Mac's core markets are still graphics, Web design, film and video production, audio, and multimedia.

So who uses Macs in business? Well, if you look in the front office of graphic design studios, Web design firms, film and video productions studios, you'll find Macs doing all their office work, from running spreadsheets to crunching their financials.

I know we don't like to admit it, but business is just not where Apple is focusing its aim—hasn't been for years. That's why Apple develops products like Final Cut Pro, iMovie, iPhoto, QuickTime, and iTunes, and they spun off their single real business product— FileMaker Pro.

So even though Macs are undeniably great at running business software, they're still primarily machines for creatives, and that's the customer Apple still markets to today.

Now, all that being said, there are some traditional businesses where Macs are very popular. For example, apparently a lot of attorneys use Macs. Maybe it's because they used Macs in law school (like at Harvard). On a sign I read on the wall of my local Apple retail store, Apple claims that one out of four attorneys uses a Macintosh. I figure it must be true because if Apple is lying, with all those attorneys out there, they'd really be begging for a lawsuit, dontchathink?

Macs are also huge in education and, depending on which survey figures you go by, Macs are in either the #1 or #2 spot in the education market.

(14) Wearing Mac stuff brings out the Mac people

Want to meet some new Mac people? Wear some Apple logo stuff. This is like waving a red cape in the streets of Pamplona. When Mac users see an Apple logo—they come running—full speed, right at you. Be prepared, deftly step aside at the last minute, and they'll zoom safely by you. When they finally slow down, just ask "What kind of Mac do you use?" and the conversation will go into "autopilot" mode from there. You just need to "hook 'em" with the logo. Once you make initial contact, you've made a friend. Also, it wouldn't hurt to mention *Star Trek* at some point.

(15) Put an Apple window sticker on your car

This is actually your duty, but it helps in a lot of ways as it attracts other Mac users, who may work in your building or live in your neighborhood, and don't know that you're a Mac user. Also, it makes you special. Ask yourself this: Does Dell pack Dell stickers with every PC they sell? If they do, Dell users don't want to brag about it, because I've never seen a Dell, or Gateway, or even a Microsoft Windows sticker on anyone's car. Really, who would brag about that? It's like putting a sticker on your car that says, "I follow the crowd. I'm a lemming." But when you put an Apple sticker on your car, you're telling the world, "I think differently. I can make my own decisions. There's something better and I've found it."

Apple knows it's a cool company, and that you're going to want to shout from the mountain tops that you're a Mac user. That's why they put those two logos on every box.

(16) Closeminded people will refer to Apple as a cult

Kill these people. (Just kidding. Just a joke. Don't kill anybody. Killing is bad, etc.)

(17) Apple makes great peripherals

If Apple makes a keyboard, mouse, or just about any peripheral, it's usually very, very good—with the notable exception of the iMac "hockey-puck" mouse and keyboard. Those were clearly the work of ex-Microsoft employees who somehow infiltrated Apple's industrial design department in an ill-fated attempt to create a mouse and keyboard so clunky and awkward that they would drive

Apple out of business. Their evil plan didn't work, but it was an environmental disaster, overflowing landfills around the world with worthless iMac keyboards, and ridiculous hockey-puck mice.

However, Apple's new mouse and keyboard are superb. Apple's AirPort—a thing of beauty. In fact, historically most of their peripherals, including displays, are outstanding products and very well built. In short, if Apple builds it, it usually rocks.

(18) Don't expect a two-button mouse. Ever.

I don't know why Apple just won't release a two-button mouse, but they just flat won't. I've heard that Apple thinks a two-button mouse is too complicated for new users. That may be true, but since we know that most people who buy a Mac already have a Mac, why doesn't Apple let us choose whether we want a one-button or two-button mouse? Because everyone would choose the two-button, of course. Why? Because that's what everybody wants. Don't hold your breath for this to change. At least, in our lifetime.

(19) Steve Jobs really cares about Apple

I'll never forget a quote about Steve that so hit the nail on the head. It was by Heidi Roizen, former Apple executive, in the May 18, 1998, issue of *Business Week:* "No matter how famous Pixar becomes, Steve is known for Apple; if Apple is tarnished, Steve is tarnished." Wow! How true.

That's why when people get all crazy with the "Steve's selling us down the river" or "Steve's really messing up this time" frenzy, I tell them, "Remember. Nobody has more to lose than Steve."

Although I've never met the man, I have a tremendous amount of respect for Steve. Even though he's often portrayed as excessively demanding and sometimes downright mean, I still respect him. Why? Because he didn't have to take the job. He's a billionaire—even listed by *Fortune* as one of the richest men on the planet. Yet, he has voluntarily taken one of the absolute toughest jobs in the entire tech industry—running Apple.

It's not like running Microsoft. That's a cake job—Microsoft practically prints its own money. Running Apple has been and always will be a very tough job (thanks to the media, Microsoft, the PC market in general, and the millions of Mac users [like me] who second-guess every move Apple makes). It's not an easy job, but he took it, and he continues to be the best leader Apple's ever had. My hat's off to him.

You know what other quality Steve has that no other CEO at any major PC company has? Cool. Steve is cool. I know it sounds silly, but you have to admit it, he's just a cool guy. Excuse me, I mean "he's cool, ya know...for a billionaire."

(20) When you buy a Mac, you'll have the best-looking machine on the block, period

I can't imagine some other PC company "outdesigning" Apple. Their industrial design team is amazing. Just look at things like Apple's AirPort, or the Cube, the iBook, or the iPod. Apple flat out knows how to design hardware. Look at Mac OS X, iMovie, iTunes, or just about any of Apple's recent software apps and you'll see Apple's design genius isn't just limited to hardware. Looks *matter,* and in that department, Apple has no peer.

Well, there you have it, 20 things I wish somebody had told me when I first got into the whole Mac scene. Now that I've told you, it's your responsibility to pass on this wisdom to the next generation. To plant the seed of what will one day create a whole class of people who will grow up to hate Microsoft. Ah, it's a beautiful world, isn't it?

CHAPTER ELEVEN

The secret
of Macintosh

Y ou've come a long way, my friend. You've reached a
place that others only dare to dream of. A place where
mysteries unfold, secrets are unearthed, confidences are
broken, funds are mismanaged, privileges are abused,
videos are returned late, and others are blamed. Yes, my friends, this
is Chapter 11. Where you learn the real secret of Macintosh.

I have to make a disclaimer before we go any further. Some of the
things you're about to read you may find shocking. The language
will often be coarse and abrasive, the imagery frank and revealing.
Some of you may find many of these concepts disturbing; but to get
where Apple is today, certain things had to be done. People were
used. Lied to. Deceived. In some cases, people were asked to do
things, and wear awkwardly fitting outer-garments that some might

find cruel and objectionable. But you have to keep in mind—it was to reach a higher plane.

Now, if you're fine with believing that Apple Computer is just an extremely lucky computer company, that's okay. Close the book and consider it "read." There's no shame in admitting you don't want to tarnish the image of Apple that you have implanted in your mind. So, if you're afraid of losing sleep over hearing the truth, *the naked truth,* then close this book and go on with your gray-flannel life. No harm done. But for everyone else, you've been duly warned. You know the consequences—continue at your own risk.

What I'm about to reveal will anger many people. It will betray a confidence that has been passed directly from person to person for more than 15 years; but I think it's time it was brought out in the open.

The secret of Macintosh is that Apple Computer is actually a cult. I don't mean some cutesy cult, like people who are really into Mazda Miatas or who go to see the *Rocky Horror Picture Show* at every midnight showing. I mean a real-life cult that preys on people who have serious conflicts and struggles in their lives. Maybe a bad childhood, a failed marriage, perhaps they're living a life filled with emptiness and pain. They're at a vulnerable stage in their lives and they'll become engrossed in anything or anyone that offers them "a way out"—a sense of purpose or belonging. Steve Jobs is, and has always been, the cult leader. Even when not at Apple, he controlled the cult, much in the same way imprisoned gang leaders still control their gangs' activities from behind bars.

Although it has evolved greatly over the years, the cult is primarily founded upon the teachings of a late 19th-century Prussian poet and author Alfred Burkhalter. It was Burkhalter who wrote a paper which many believe was the precursor to the entire Apple revolution. But it was his grandson, Otto Burkhalter, who emigrated from his post-World War I home in Bern, Switzerland to Düsseldorf, Germany to continue his grandfather's work, decades before anyone had even thought of modern computers.

Otto went on to compose what is known to Apple cult members today as "The underground Macintosh manifesto"—thought by many to be the blueprint Steve Jobs used to form his Apple cult some forty years later.

Sadly, Burkhalter's work was never completed because of Germany's entry into World War II, and his subsequent service in the German Army.

Herr Burkhalter eventually became a general in the German Army, and wound up in charge of several World War II military prison camps where U.S. and other Allied prisoners of war were held.

General Burkhalter would often visit these camps and threaten the commanding officer (the Kommandant) of the camp, and his second-in-command, Sergeant Schultz—usually because either Lebeau or Col. Hogan had escaped through an underground tunnel, and was caught drinking with the *fräuleins* in Berlin. He would yell things like, "Klink! I'm sending you to the front!" and other threats of military discipline. You're not really buying any of this crap, are you? Because honestly, I'm just making it up as I go (partially to illustrate a point, and partially as a tribute to *Hogan's Heroes*). By the way, if history is any indicator, some PC journalist will take segments of this cobbled-up story and use it as the basis of an investigative report that will gain nationwide attention.

Whatever the mainstream media, and magazines like *Forbes,* would like you to believe, there is no "Cult of Macintosh." No secret handshakes, no robes, no blood oaths; and although Steve Jobs has a lot of charisma, is Apple's leader and a genius, he is not a "charismatic evil genius."

Headlines and news pieces about the "Cult of Macintosh" sell magazines and newspapers, because people that don't "get Apple" think that's the only explanation of why millions would voluntarily choose something other than a beige PC running Windows. It just doesn't make sense to them that people would care for a company the way people do about Apple, and that people would fall in love with a company's product the way people do with a Macintosh. Really, when you think about this, it's sad. It's sad how closeminded we've become as a society, and how brainwashed we've been to accept second best.

There *is* a secret to Macintosh, and there is a secret to Apple and their seemingly unexplainable success. We'll start with Apple. The secret to Apple's success is "you." Plain and simple, it's you. The person reading this book. If you're reading this book, I can almost guarantee you this—Apple owes you. Why? Because you sell Macintosh computers. You are probably among Apple's top sales people, and the real reason why Apple is such a success.

Let's face it, although Apple's advertising under Steve Jobs is probably the best it's ever been, for most of Apple's history many people would agree that it fell somewhere between an absolute joke and a total disgrace. So what kept Apple afloat all those years? We did, you did, I did. Our friends did. How? By getting our families and friends to buy Macs.

I'll give you an example. Back in the late '80s I bought my first Mac. A few years later I bought my wife her first Mac. Not long after, my brother bought his first Mac and my best friend, John Couch, bought his first Mac. Before long, my brother bought his second Mac, and not too long afterward my dad bought his first Mac. Soon my brother bought a Mac for his office, and one of his best friends bought a Mac. His next girlfriend bought a Mac, and his current girlfriend uses nothing but Macs. When my son was 2 years old, he got his first Mac (a tangerine iMac), and now he also uses an iBook.

Years ago, I convinced my friend Jim Workman to buy a Mac. Jim bought his wife a Mac, his mother a Mac, some Macs for his old business, and dozens of Macs for his current business. He bought his brother a Mac and his 7-year-old son Kevin has an iMac, too.

With never a sales commission being paid, without a single kickback or even a thank you, we've all become the best, most enthusiastic, tireless, well-trained sales force the computing world has ever seen. We sell Macintosh computers by the truckload, every day, all around the world! We sell them to our families, our most trusted friends, new acquaintances, anyone who will listen. We are a wildly motivated sales force that makes the best Amway reps look passive and disinterested by comparison.

Why do we do it? This is going to sound silly, but we do it because we know it's going to make people happy, and that makes us happy. I know, that sounds very "touchy-feely," but I honestly believe that's why we do it—because making someone's life better makes us happy.

Here's an example of what I mean: My Brother Jeff loves to travel in Europe. Over the years, he had been to Paris a number of times, and really loved the city. Back in 1983 he was going to Paris again and was nice enough to invite me to go with him. After we arrived in Paris, he really wanted to take me on le Métro (their name for a subway) and get off at a specific stop near the Champs Élysées. His reason was that when you came up the steps from this particular Métro stop to the street level, the awe-inspiring l'Arc de Triomphe was standing majestically before you. He thought it was really breathtaking and moving, and he wanted me to have that same thrill. He made sure he got up the Métro stairs before I did, so he could see my face as I saw the architectural marvel for the first time.

As you might have guessed, when I saw it I was absolutely speechless. But somehow, I think my brother got more out of it than I did. That's because he got to share something with me that had been very special for him. Seeing my reaction, knowing that he had shared his special moment with me, made him happy. I guarantee he can remember the moment that he brought me to l'Arc de Triomphe as clearly as the day he saw it himself for the first time.

Some years later, I was the first one up those Métro stairs, and was lucky enough to see my soon-to-be wife come up that very same staircase. Watching her see l'Arc de Triomphe for the first time actually brought a tear to my eyes, as I got to share that very special moment with her. That made me very, very happy. This is what I'm talking about.

Getting to share the wonder of Macintosh with someone you care about is (corny as this may sound) very special. You've found something that you think is wonderful, unique, fascinating, even exciting; and you want to tell everyone you can and share this special news. You want to relive that moment when you "got it." When you realized this is more than just another dumb computer. It's something special. Every time you turn someone on to the Mac, and you see them "get it," it makes you feel good inside. You just helped someone. It's like telling somebody about a great little restaurant, or a special deal at a store that nobody knows about. You've shared something to make someone happy, without any personal gain except the feeling that you did something good for somebody. That's pretty damn neat.

What's the other half?

So now you know half of the story—the secret to Apple's success— which is having the world's largest, best-trained, most motivated, unpaid sales force. Now, what's the other half—what is the rest of the secret to Macintosh? What is so friggin' great about the Macintosh, that otherwise perfectly sane people will go against the grain, willingly turn away from computers that are more popular, offer tons more software, more peripherals, more support, more variety, and yet actually cost less money to buy? The secret of the Macintosh is (drum roll, please…) the Mac's sheer simplicity. It is, plain and simple, the easiest computer on the planet to learn, use, and maintain. Anyone can learn to use a Macintosh. Anyone. And that same person will be able to connect a Zip drive, a scanner, and a digital camcorder, without any previous computing experience.

For example: When you buy a Mac printer, on the end of the cable is a little icon of a printer. To find out where the printer plugs into your Mac, just look at the back of your Mac to find the matching jack. That's it. That's the way it's always been. No instructions. No engineering degree necessary. Match the little icon on the cord to the little icon on your Mac, and it's connected. That's the way the

Macintosh has been designed from the ground up. You plug it in, and it works. First time. On the Macintosh, plug-and-play is a way of life—always has been.

One of the best visual manifestations of the simplicity of the Macintosh I ever experienced was at Macworld Expo when Apple introduced its iMovie software for making your own movies. Two long rows of iMacs were set up in the Apple pavilion, and attached to the wall behind each iMac was a digital camcorder. It was connected to the iMac and turned on, so if you walked up to the iMac you'd see yourself on its screen. People were standing two and three deep to walk up and try iMovie themselves.

There was no instruction manual. No training video. No instructions of any kind and people were right there making movies (with themselves as the stars). When it was my turn, before I realized it, I too was making movies. Totally without help, guidance, or instruction of any kind. I was adding titles, transitions, effects, and I fell in love with it right on the spot—it was brilliant. So there we were, in the middle of 80,000 people on a crowded show floor, row upon row of us making our first iMovies, all on our own. That is the power of the Mac's simplicity at its best. Powerful software that is so easy, so intuitive, so user-friendly that it doesn't need an instruction manual.

So why does this stuff all work so well together? Why does plug-and-play work so perfectly on a Mac, when on a PC it's more like "plug-and-pray?" Why is the software so easy to learn on a Mac, but on a PC, each new program has a separate learning curve? It's because Apple makes both the hardware and the operating system; therefore, it has control.

It has clear standards for Mac software and hardware developers, and to develop for the Macintosh platform, you have to follow Apple's standards.

Here's a classic case in point: Since the very beginning, Apple has made it a standard that the word software developers would use to quit a Macintosh software program would be "Quit." Always. The keyboard shortcut must *always* be Command-Q, and the place where Quit must appear in *every* Mac software package is as the last item in the File menu. That's the rule, and that's the way it works to this very day. So when you install a new program for the very first time, without ever reading the instruction manual, you already know how to Quit, what the keyboard shortcut is, and where to find it in the new program's menus.

However, on the PC there is no absolute set of rules developers *must* follow, so they can use any word they want to quit a program—Exit, End, Stop, Escape, Get me outta here, Leave, Shut Down—it's up to the individual developer (though many now follow Apple's lead and just use Quit). They can also use any keyboard shortcut they want, and place the command under any menu they desire, leaving you to figure out how to quit each program. It sounds silly, and it is.

Okay, so it's easier. But how much easier?

My favorite example of "how much easier" is the "Ultimate Mac versus Windows Challenge" that was conducted at the 1996 Software Publisher's Association Conference in San Francisco. The SPA's idea was to pit two teams against each other in a head-to-head competition to find out which computing platform was easier to use.

A team of Mac users and a team of Windows users would each perform a series of real-world tasks indicative of what a typical consumer might experience. Each team would start with a new computer (still in the box) then set it up, install a modem, connect a Zip drive, get onto the Internet, connect to a network, create a file, save it, make an alias (or shortcut) to it, and finally uninstall an application. All of this would be performed on stage in front of a live audience.

Apple accepted the SPA's invitation to participate and Apple Evangelist Guy Kawasaki assembled a team to represent the Macintosh side. Microsoft was invited to send a team, but declined; so the SPA recruited both the Editor-in-Chief of *Windows Sources* magazine and his assistant to be the Windows team.

The Windows team was introduced and took the stage. But when the Macintosh team was announced, just one person took the stage—a 10-year-old boy named Alex Stein. That's right, Alex would complete all the real-world tests himself against the team of PC experts from *Windows Sources* magazine. In an undeniable testament to the ease of using Macintosh, young Alex easily beat the team of Windows pros in nearly every category. We should also note that during the contest, the PC crashed six times, while the Macintosh never crashed at all.

That's what the public saw. But what the audience didn't see was perhaps even more impressive. Guy noted that the Macintosh system was brand-new, still factory-sealed in the box. The PC system was also new; but prior to the live contest, the box was unsealed and the system assembled and tested in advance by the *Windows Sources* editor. After his testing, he reportedly returned the computer to a "virgin state." Guy also learned that during this "pre-show testing," the *Window Sources* editor spent nearly two hours on the phone with tech support because he couldn't get the printer to work.

This gives you just a tiny glimpse into the world of complexity that PC users face every day. But these were PC experts, not average everyday users. If *they* had to spend hours on the phone with tech support just to get the printer to work, what would the average consumer's experience be like? Even though this happened a few years back, in the previous chapter you just read excerpts from *PC World* magazine indicating that not much has changed since then—experts are still struggling with things that should be simple everyday tasks.

Apple was apparently inspired by the success of the "Ultimate Mac versus PC Challenge" because in 1998 they produced a QuickTime movie to show how insanely easy the iMac is to set up and connect to the Internet. This one was called the "Simplicity shoot-out," and like the live contest, each team would set up a computer system and connect to the Internet. Representing Apple was 7-year-old Johann Thomas, but he had help—he was assisted by his pet dog, Brodie. Representing the PC side was Adam Taggart, a 26-year-old Stanford University MBA. Johann would set up an Apple iMac; Adam would set up a Hewlett-Packard PC system. As you might imagine, Adam (and Brodie) easily whipped the Stanford MBA. The clip is absolutely hilarious, but more importantly, it drives home the Mac's "ease of use" advantage in such a clear, visual, and amusing way.

She says it better than I ever could

The fact that the Macintosh is easier is really no big secret. That's been well documented over the years in independent study after boring independent study. It's *how much* easier, and more trouble-free the Macintosh is to use that makes all the difference.

Because the learning stage doesn't really take that long, before you know it, you're very comfortable with the Mac and how it operates. The other part of the "Secret of Macintosh" is that once you become accustomed to using a Mac, you'll find out that Macs are also *so* much easier to maintain. People are more productive on a Mac, get more work done, and spend more time creating and less time troubleshooting their machines, thanks to Apple's one-two punch of designing both the hardware and the system software.

But how tough are things really for PC users? One of my all-time favorite quotes comes from an article I read in April '98 issue of *PC World* magazine. It was from Cathryn Baskin, then *PC World's* Editor-in-Chief. She was lamenting a number of problems, including a horror story her friend experienced trying to install a game for her son on his PC. After detailing the problems her friend had encountered, she wrote, "PC hardware and software problems are so common that we've come to accept them as normal." She closes the article with the rhetorical question, "Who would tolerate these sorts of problems with cars, TVs, or telephones?" Obviously, the problems she speaks of are the norm on the PC platform, not the exception to the rule; but as she points out, PC users have learned to accept them as normal. Amazing, isn't it?

Have you noticed that you don't read articles in any of the
Macintosh magazines about how often Macs crash, or nightmares
of installations, endless incompatibility problems, or stories of how
Mac experts spent days simply trying to get their system to work?
Not that it's never happened. Mac problems do happen. It's just that
they happen so infrequently that if a Mac magazine ran an article
like that, its readers wouldn't be able to relate. That's because for the
most part, those never-ending technical nightmares simply don't
exist. That is part of what makes a Macintosh truly magic.

Day-to-day living with a PC

So how productive are PC users once they actually get their PCs up
and running? Well, take a look at the best-selling business titles for
the PC platform. I remember *Windows* magazine running a list of
the top 10 best-selling Windows software titles, and eight of the top
ten bestsellers were either anti-virus protection programs or crash-
recovery programs. That's right, the overwhelming majority of the
top-selling Windows apps were utilities designed either to help PC
users keep their PCs running, or to recover from their crashes when
they weren't. Pretty scary stuff.

Unsolicited testimonials

As a Mac user, have you ever watched another Mac user doing what
you know as a simple one-step task, but you see them doing it the
hard way? Maybe using 15 steps to do what you do in just one
keyboard shortcut? So you lean over and whisper, "Did you know if
you hold the Command key, it will do all that for you in just one
step?" They generally drop their jaw and exclaim, "Oh my God,

you're kidding me! That's all I need to do? Do you know how many times a day I do that? I can't believe I've been doing it the hard way all this time!"

This is *exactly* the same type of reaction you'll hear from a PC user who's switched to Macintosh. It's really a treat to meet someone just a few months after they've made the switch. They're absolutely glowing. It's as if they've unraveled a mystery of life and they can finally see clearly. They'll tell you, "I had no idea the Mac was like this!" and invariably they blame Apple for not letting the world know about this "secret." Because surely if the world really knew how easy, fun, and virtually trouble-free the Macintosh is, they'd switch from the PC platform in a heartbeat.

If you ever want to meet a real, honest-to-goodness, raving Macintosh lunatic, it's someone who's switched from Windows to the Mac. That person is hands-down the best unpaid salesperson Apple will ever have.

The other thing you'll invariably hear from a converted Windows user is that they can't believe so many millions of PC users are still stuck, battling every day with the problems and sheer complexity of the PC platform when their lives could be so much easier, "if they only knew."

That…that right there, is the real "Secret of Macintosh." It's so vastly easier to learn, use, and maintain that it actually makes your life better. By using a Macintosh, you completely sidestep a nasty and tremendously time-consuming side of computing that PC users have to struggle with every day, and that they think is normal. This enables you to get more work done, which makes you more productive and less stressed out, and gives you a chance to do something that I believe most PC users rarely get to do—enjoy their computer. That's sad, because that may be what separates Mac users and PC users the most. Mac users truly enjoy their computer because they really know the difference, and the secret.

One last thing

I want to put your mind at ease about Apple Computer as a company. Do what I do, "Don't worry about Apple." The best way I've ever heard it expressed was during my first trip to Apple's Cupertino headquarters a few years back, while Apple was going through one of its rough periods (before Steve's return). I got off the plane at the San Jose airport, and as I was heading toward baggage claim I noticed a large backlit ad on the terminal wall. What caught my eye was the Apple logo at the bottom of the ad. I walked over and saw that it was an ad recruiting people to join Apple as employees. Since it was a local employment ad, maybe that's why I've never, before or since, read the quote that I'm going to share with you. At the bottom of the ad, this said it all:

"There will always be skeptics.
There will always be disbelievers.
And there will always be Apple to prove them wrong."

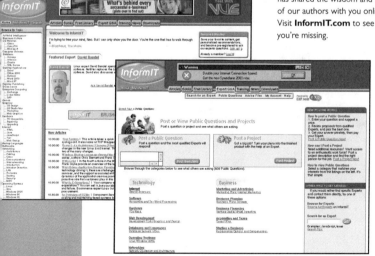

VOICES THAT MATTER

HOW TO CONTACT US

VISIT OUR WEB SITE AT WWW.NEWRIDERS.COM

On our web site, you'll find information about our other books, authors, tables of contents, and book errata. You will also find information about book registration and how to purchase our books, both domestically and internationally.

EMAIL US

Contact us at: **nrfeedback@newriders.com**

- If you have comments or questions about this book
- To report errors that you have found in this book
- If you have a book proposal to submit or are interested in writing for New Riders
- If you are an expert in a computer topic or technology and are interested in being a technical editor who reviews manuscripts for technical accuracy

Contact us at: **nreducation@newriders.com**

- If you are an instructor from an educational institution who wan to preview New Riders books for classroom use. Email should include your name, title, school, department, address, phone number, office days/hours, text in use, and enrollment, along with your request for desk/examination copies and/or additional information.

Contact us at: **nrmedia@newriders.com**

- If you are a member of the media who is interested in reviewing copies of New Riders books. Send your name, mailing address, a email address, along with the name of the publication or Web sit you work for.

BULK PURCHASES/CORPORATE SALES

If you are interested in buying 10 or more copies of a title or want to set up an account for your company to purchase directly from the publisher at a substantial discount, contact us at 800-382-3419 or email your contact information to corpsales@pearsontechgroup.com. A sales representative will contact you with more information.

WRITE TO US

New Riders Publishing
201 W. 103rd St.
Indianapolis, IN 46290-1097

CALL/FAX US

Toll-free (800) 571-5840
If outside U.S. (317) 581-3500
Ask for New Riders
FAX: (317) 581-4663

New
Riders

WWW.NEWRIDERS.C